The Illiad, The Odyssey, and All of Greek Mythology in 99 minutes or less

Jay Hopkins
and John Hunter

A Samuel French Acting Edition

SAMUEL FRENCH
FOUNDED 1830

SAMUELFRENCH.COM
SAMUELFRENCH-LONDON.CO.UK

Cover Art by Gene Sweeney

ISBN 978-0-573-66387-1
www.SamuelFrench.com
www.SamuelFrench-London.co.uk

For Production Enquiries

United States and Canada
Info@SamuelFrench.com
1-866-598-8449

United Kingdom and Europe
Theatre@SamuelFrench-London.co.uk
020-7255-4302

Each title is subject to availability from Samuel French, depending upon country of performance. Please be aware that *THE ILIAD, THE ODYSSEY, AND ALL OF GREEK MYTHOLOGY IN 99 MINUTES OR LESS* may not be licensed by Samuel French in your territory. Professional and amateur producers should contact the nearest Samuel French office or licensing partner to verify availability.

PLAYWRIGHT BIOS

JAY HOPKINS has been an actor, improvisor, director and producer in Orlando, Florida since 1989. He has created and directed several improvisational based shows including FOOLISH HEARTS, CAPTAIN GOODNESS VS. THE INJUSTICE LEAGUE, and AUDITION, which were produced at the SAK Theatre Comedy Lab, where he was Artistic Producer and a member of the company since 1992. Jay is currently the founder and Artistic Director of the Jester Theater Company in Orlando Florida.

JOHN HUNTER is an Emeritus member of the Writer's Guild of America. He was a staff writer for the Showtime television series RUDE AWAKENING, and UPN's series GROWN-UPS. Other notable work include: contributions to Comedy Central's THE MAN SHOW; POLITICALLY INCORRECT WITH BILL MAHER; and optioned screenplays with New Line Cinema and Fox 2000 Studios. He currently works as Associate Artistic Director of the SAK Theatre Comedy Lab in Orlando, Florida.

Jay and John have known each other and performed together since 1992. Together, they have written for the sketch comedy shows TRENDY BRITCHES and CONTENTS UNDER PRESSURE, as well as the Orlando International Fringe Festival favorite NEARSIGHTED JUSTICE, the improvised courtroom comedy that had its extended run at SAK Theatre Comedy Lab.

THE ILIAD, THE ODYSSEY & ALL OF GREEK MYTHOLOGY IN 99 MINUTES OR LESS was first produced by Diana Hopkins and The Jester Theater Company at the Studio Theatre on March 2, 2007, in Orlando, Florida. The performance was directed by Jay Hopkins, with sets and sound design by Jay Hopkins, costumes by Alea Schroeder, lilghting by Charles Downs, and props by Alea Schroeder and Diana Hopkins. The Production Stage Manager was Jennifer Russo. The cast was as follows:

M1 . . . . Ryan Gigliotti
M2 . . . . Jamie Cline
M3 . . . . Chase Padgett
F1 . . . . Jamie Bridwell
F2 . . . . Gina DiRoma

THE SETTING

The stage is a unit set with areas represented as necessary. A couple of risers, Greek columns, benches, a chair, a few props (necessary for onstage character changes) and a timer.

THE SCENES

The scenes are indicated in Bold throughout the script but change fluidly from one to the next, with maybe only a light change to indicate the new scene.

THE ROLES

The actors will play multiple roles, switching back and forth as necessary. Actors will play the same characters throughout the show (see character breakdown). Roles do NOT switch from actor to actor.

This script is written for 5 actors (3M, 2F) for the most fun, but can be cast in any combination, and if more actors are cast, roles can be divided accordingly by the director.

CHARACTER BREAKDOWN

Since casting is very flexible, here is a description of the types best suited for the roles as they are divided now.

M1 – The more mature and masculine of the three men. A feeling of authority and dignity will help this actor. Key roles are Zeus and Achilles, Old Nestor, Perseus and Old Dog.

M2 – The more impulsive and eager of the three men. His emotional rawness and passion play large parts in his characters. Key roles are Odysseus, Hector and Hera.

M3 – The goofiest and more cartoon-like of the three men. Natural comedic skills are a major plus for this actor playing so many different character parts. Key roles are Hermes, Man, Paris, Agamemnon, Diomedes and Hercules.

F1 – The more mature of the two women. A solid actress with the ability to show wounded emotions and dignity. Key roles are Athena, Demeter, Ms. Henderson, Patroklos and Oracle.

F2 – The more ingénue of the two women. Youthfulness is a help but she still plays older as well. Key roles are Aphrodite, Pandora, Helen of Troy and Old King Priam.

Actors will each play 18 to 32 characters as listed on the chart in the back of the script.

SCENIC OUTLINE

Act I

A – Opening / Creation / Titan War
B – The Gods
C – The Creation of Mankind
D – Pandora
E – The Earth Goddess - Demeter & Persephone
F – The Earth God - Dionysus w/ Zeus & Semele
G – Greek Chorus of the Madwomen
H – Love Stories, Pt. 1
I – The Wedding that started it all & the Apple of Discord
J – Paris kidnaps Helen /Menelaos and Agamemnon call to war
K – Oracle / Agamemnon gets Achilles and Odysseus

THE ILIAD:

Book 1 – Achilles gets screwed by Agamemnon
Book 2 – False dream / rally speech
Book 3 – Paris challenges Menelaos
Book 4 – Hera sends Athena to Pandaros the Archer
Book 5 – Diomedes Rules w/ Athena's help
Book 6 – Diomedes & Glaukos / Hector, Helen & Paris
Book 7 – Choosing warriors / Ajax vs. Hector +Antenor
Book 8 – Iris messenger
Book 9 – Odysseus tries to reason w/ Achilles
Book 10 – Odysseus & Diomedes night raid
Book 11 – Diomedes wounded by Paris / Cooking pot
Book 12 – Trojan omens
Book 13 – Poseidon tries to help / Odysseus loses the keys
Book 14 – (just a lot of arguing)
Book 15 – Patroklos confers w/ Nestor
Book 16 – Patroklos gets armor and gets killed
Book 17 – Menelaos and the gun
Book 18 – Achilles tries monologuing/Thetis + Hephaestus
Book 19 – Achilles returns to fight / Noble steed
Book 20 – Zeus sends the Gods to war
Book 21 – The Brawl by the Wall
Book 22 – The Battle
Book 23 – (A dream and a funeral)
Book 24 – The Final Book – Hermes & Priam sent to reason w/ Achilles

Act II

A – The Love Stories, Pt. 2
B – Greek Idol Pt. 1 / Jason, Perseus, Theseus
C – The Poker Game
D – Greek Idol Pt. 2 / Phaethon, Hercules
E – Houses of Tragedy
F – Greek Idol Pt. 3 / Odysseus wins
G – The Trojan Horse

THE ODYSSEY:

H – The Odyssey begins
I – The Cyclops
J – The Land of the Wind
K – Circe of the Enchantress
L – Land of the Dead
M – The Choices
N – Calypso
O – The Phaecians
P – The Final Journey Home
Q – Father/Son reunion
R – Suitors & Old Dog
S – The Plan and the Prayers
T – Slaughter in the Hall
U – The Great Bed
V – The Ending

PRODUCTION NOTES
FROM JAY HOPKINS AND JOHN HUNTER:

1) Obviously, this show could be cast with more actors (taking a lot of the fun out of it...for you AND the audience, in our opinion). We did this with three men and two women, with men and women playing male AND female roles. If you wish to cast differently, that's your business. You have our permission. Let us know how it works out.

2) This is a PROP HEAVY show. In order for the actors to play multiple roles quickly, (sometimes switching onstage, back and forth between three roles in three or four consecutive lines), we needed to find one or two costume pieces or props that could identify a character immediately [For example: Zeus always carried a lightning bolt; Achilles carried a dumbbell when he wasn't fighting; Odysseus just wears glasses. These pieces were added to the base toga costumes.] Again, if you have the budget and costume crew to use more elaborate changes, that's your business. Let us know how it works out.

3) Obviously, this is a silly show. Please have lots and lots of fun doing it! Don't take yourself too seriously. That doesn't mean mug, comment or do unnecessary takes to the audience. That will come off as begging for laughs. Audiences don't like that. They will much prefer you give it your earnest attention.

We found the longer a character is onstage, the stronger and less cartoony it needs to be. The less time onstage, the more silly it can be. Dialects, accents, impressions, caricatures, whatever take you want to do, just be certain that they are distinct enough...because you'll confuse the audience if you're not solid in all the parts. The costume accessories will only help, but the portrayal of each character makes the difference.

4) The clock. If you put a clock onstage...the audience will watch it. You don't have to, but it is part of the fun. We'd prefer an actual timer of 99 minutes that an audience can see, can be stopped by the cast, and sounds a bell or buzzer when time is up.

We couldn't find a 90 minute timer (original title of the show... *Il, Od & All...in 90 minutes or less*). We actually had a kitchen timer set for 60 minutes and then added the time after the intermission, in front of the audience to make 90 minutes total. If the timer went off at 60 minutes and the first act was still going on, either Zeus or Hermes would step into the scene and say, "I'm a God. I command more time." and then added time as appropriate. The Ml actor would just set the timer off at the end of the show for the final bell and cast sigh. Whatever solution you come up with, we'd like to know.

5) Pacing is everything. This show moves. Actors need to be predictive with entrances and exits and character switches. They need to be on each others heels. This does NOT mean say lines so fast that you lose meaning, comic timing or intent. Pick up your cues, don't speed through your lines. Trust us: it will all sound the same and then the drone will bore your audience.

for Dorkus McGorkus and Piso Mojado...
and to Angela, of course.

ACT I

The Opening

(The stage is bare, except for a couple of benches and a timer of some sort. **M1** *enters the stage at a deliberate and unhurried pace. He walks to the timer so the audience can see and sets it running for 99 minutes. He steps forward.)*

M1. *(calmly)* Hello, and welcome to…

(Instantly, **F1** *runs onstage with a panicked look!)*

F1. *(shouting backstage)* Oh My God HE STARTED THE CLOCK!

ALL OFFSTAGE. He WHAT!???!

(**M2** *runs onstage.)*

M2. STOP IT FOR GOD'S SAKE! No one told us we were starting!

(**F1** *stops* **M2** *from stopping clock, leading him offstage.* **M1** *exits as* **F2** *enters.)*

M1. I thought we should welcome the…

F1. No time! Let's GO!!!

The Creation

F2. The Creation! In the beginning there was only chaos until a wind born egg begat Mother Earth, who was called Gaea…so we'll call her Gaea. And Father Heaven, who was called Uranus, so we'll call him... Father Heaven, because I can't even say Uranus with a straight face.

Their children were Monsters and Cyclopses and Titans. Father Heaven hated the Monsters, which upset Mother Earth very much, so she begged her child Cronus to help her. Cronus wounded Father Heaven terribly, and from his blood sprang the Giants...and the Eagles, and the Broncos, and of course the Furies, whose job was to punish the sinners.

Anyway, Titan Cronus became ruler of the universe and that is the story of the creation…part 1.

The Titan War

(M3 *enters.*)

M3. Part 2! So, Cronus was ruling the Universe after wounding Uranus…

ALL OFFSTAGE VOICES. Ewww!

M3. After wounding Father Heaven, Cronus found out that one of his children was destined to dethrone him. So he swallowed all his children as soon as they were born.

When his wife-slash-sister-slash-queen Rhea caught on, after the first *five* children, she snuck the baby Zeus away to Crete. When Zeus was grown, there was a big battle between Cronus and Zeus. The monsters fought on the side of Zeus with weapons of thunder, lightning and earthquake and atomic wedgies, and Zeus won.

Zeus punished Cronus by binding him in chains and banishing him to Tartarus, the land of decay and plaque build up. He forced Atlas, who fought alongside Cronus, to bear the weight of Heaven and Earth on his shoulders.

Zeus and the Greek Gods now ruled the Universe.

The Gods

(**M2** *enters.*)

M2. Programs! Programs! Can't do the myths if you don't know the Gods! And you won't know the Gods without a program! Getcha' programs right here!

We give you your starting lineup of the Tweeeeelllllllve Greeeeeaaatttt Olympians!!!!!! Starting with the Head of the Olympians: stronger than all the remaining Greek Gods combined; he wields the mighty thunderbolt; his bird is the eagle and his tree the mighty oak. He's got grandeur, he's got glory…heeeere's ZEUS!

*(***ZEUS** *[***M1***] enters proudly with* **JANE** *[***F1***].* **M2** *exits.)*

M1-ZEUS. Thank you, thank you, and thank you.

F1-JANE. No, thank you. So Zeus…big reputation to live up to tonight. How do you feel about tonight's show?

M1-ZEUS. Wow, Jane. That's a good question. You know, I'm not ALL powerful. I can be tricked or fooled. *(with false modesty)* I'm just a God. Tonight, I'm looking to tell a few good stories. I'd just like to have some fun and maybe meet a few women…and if that means making an animal out of myself, then so be it!

F1-JANE. Thanks Zeus. We're all looking forward to seeing you, whatever you look like.

*(***ZEUS** *exits.)*

Next up for the Olympians we've got a real tough cookie. Born the "cow-faced" daughter of Titan Cronus, she's the sister AND the wife of Zeus. She's the protector of marriage. The cow and the peacock are sacred to her. Here she comes. It's HERA!!!

*(***HERA** *[***M2***] enters wearing a cow nose.)*

M2-HERA. Were you flirting with Zeus? I swear if you were I'll smite you.

F1-JANE. No, no, honest. Hera, could we talk about tonight?

M2-HERA. Oh, sure. I'm just going to keep my eye on Zeus and step in when I'm needed. Oh, and I'd like to say "hi" to my daughter Ilithyia. She couldn't be here tonight because she's helping women in childbirth. Hi baby!

F1-JANE. Good for her! Good luck tonight.

(**HERA** *exits.)*

Next up for the Greek squad: Zeus's brothers. First, of course, he's the tide shaper and the wave-maker, commonly called the "Earth-shaker." And his brother; elusive, mysterious, hard to see because of his helmet of invisibility. Please welcome the Lord of the Sea and the King of the Dead…POSEIDON AND HADES!!!!!!!!!!

(**POSEIDON** *[***M1***] and* **HADES** *[***M2***] enter.* **POSEIDON** *carries his trident and is a fun- loving crowd-pleasing surfer dude.* **HADES** *carries the helmet of invisibility on a stick.)*

M1-POSEIDON. Woooo!!! How's it going sea lovers!!!!! It's great to be me. Let me tell you…Zeus, Hades and me, we drew lots! Are you kidding me!?! I got the seas! I got my hot bride Amphitrite and I got an awesome palace! I ROCK!!!! Check me out world!!! *(starts twirling his trident martial arts style)* Awesome!!!!!

(**POSEIDON** *will play in the background, then exit.* **M2** *steps in as Hades voice, then actually as Hades when he takes off the helmet.)*

F1-JANE. *(talking to empty helmet)* And here we have Death himself, Hades! How are you tonight?

M2-HADES VOICE. Not to nitpick, but I am not Death… that's Thanatos. I am the *King* of the Dead.

F1-JANE. Rumor has it you're an eligible bachelor. Any chance of taking off that helmet of invisibility to let the ladies see you?

(He does, revealing a goofy face.)

OOH! Well, good luck on finding that special someone!

*(**HADES** exits.)*

Now we're going to go to Tom. Who have you found Tom?

*(**JANE** exits for quick change to **ATHENA. TOM** [**M1**] enters.)*

M1-TOM. Thanks, Jane. This next goddess is the daughter of Zeus, the "gray-eyed" Goddess of warfare and wisdom. The owl is her bird, the olive (created by her) is her tree and Athens is her city. Please welcome… ATHENA!

*(**ATHENA** [**F1**] enters.)*

Good Evening, Athena. Is there any truth to the rumors of your birth?

F1-ATHENA. Yes, Tom, it's true. I sprang out of my father's head, fully grown, dressed in armor. I guess that's why I'm his favorite.

M1-TOM. Talk about a Caesarian!

F1-ATHENA. Actually, Caesar is Roman. I'm Greek. I'm the only one Daddy trusts to carry his thunderbolts.

M1-TOM. Fascinating!

F1-ATHENA. Now, I know I can be a bit war-like, but don't think of me as unfeminine. I only get that way when I am defending the state and home from outside enemies.

M1-TOM. And when dealing with Paris of Troy.

F1-ATHENA. Hey, he had it coming!

(She exits.)

M1-TOM. Ooooh! Foreshadowing the Iliad! Moving on. These next two Olympians are twin siblings of the fruitful Zeus and their mother, the Titan Leto. They are the gods of the sun and moon respectively. Let's here it for APOLLO AND ARTEMIS!!!!!!!!! Thank you both for coming.

*(**APOLLO** [**M2**] and **ARTEMIS** [**F2**] enter. He wears a laurel wreath, carries his golden lyre and is calm and well-mannered. She has a bow and arrow and is a bit on*

the wild, uncivilized side. She is tracking something.)

M2-APOLLO. Thank you for hosting us this evening. The pleasure is all ours.

F2-ARTEMIS. Sssshhhhhh.

*(**ARTEMIS** sees something offstage, aims and shoots her bow and arrow, clearly hits something and runs off to get whatever it is she has shot.)*

M1-TOM. Apollo, look. Your lyre!

M2-APOLLO. Lyre? I'm the God of Truth.

M1-TOM. No. I mean your harp! I bet our audience would love a song!

*(As Apollo speaks his next line, a **ROADIE** [**M3**] runs out and places an amp next to him and hands him the cord to plug in, which he does w/o even looking.)*

M2-APOLLO. Well, I didn't really prepare anything.

(SFX- Rock guitar bend down followed by the opening notes of a blazing rendition of "Stairway to Olympus.")

M1-TOM. *(cutting him off almost instantly)* Oh, I'm sorry, we're running short on time. Thanks so much though. Let's give him a hand everyone.

*(**ROADIE** strikes amp. **TOM** gently pushes **APOLLO** out.)*

M2-APOLLO. Thank you. If you'd like to book me, I'm available for parties. Just call my oracle in Delphi.

*(As **APOLLO** makes his gracious exit, **ARTEMIS** reappears carrying her prey and ready to hunt more. **TOM** reels her in.)*

M1-TOM. Thank you…oh look! Here she is, the Goddess of the Moon, protectress of young women. Any advice for the folks watching?

F2-ARTEMIS. Uhm…Be good to the cypress trees and wild animals…especially the deer, OK? So fine, can I go… your cologne smells like a three-headed dog marked his territory on you.

M1-TOM. *(embarrassed, slyly smelling himself)* Sure thing. Good luck to you. Let's go back to Jane.

*(**ARTEMIS** exits for quick change to Aphrodite. **TOM** exits. **JANE** [**F1**] enters.)*

F1-JANE. Thanks Tom! With our next goddess comes beauty. The myrtle is her tree, the dove is her bird. Straight from the sea-foam, let's give some love to the lovely laughter loving Goddess of Love and Beauty... APHRODITE!!!!!

*(**APHRODITE** [**F2**] enters wearing Greek letters, Alpha Rho Delta* (ΑΡΔ). *She is giggling and not unlike a spoiled sorority girl.)*

F2-APHRODITE. Oh , Hi!!!! Hey, where's the party?

*(Offstage we hear **HEPHAESTUS**.)*

M3-HEPHAESTUS VOICE OFFSTAGE. Aphrodite? Sweetheart? Where are you?

*(**HEPHAESTUS** [**M3**] enters fully a geek with horn rimmed glasses taped at the bridge and Vulcan ears.)*

M3-HEPHAESTUS. There you are my one true love.

F1-JANE. Ladies and Gentleman, this is Mr. Aphrodite, the God of Fire himself, Hephaestus.

M3-HEPHAESTUS. Uhm, actually, she's Mrs. Hephae...

F2-APHRODITE. *(annoyed, aside to **HEPHAESTUS**)* What do you want?

M3-HEPHAESTUS. What, oh, right. *(trying to be firm)* Sweetheart, for this anniversary, which ONE do you want... A diamond, an emerald, or a ruby?

F2-APHRODITE. *(putting on the charm instantly)* Could I have one of each?

M3-HEPHAESTUS. *(caving instantly)* Anything for you my angelic pearl.

F2-APHRODITE. Oh! And pearls too!

*(**HEPHAESTUS** exits happy as an oyster shell.)*

F1-JANE. Wow, Aphrodite, that was quite impressive.

F2-APHRODITE. I know, thanks. It's not that hard actually.

He was coddled way too much by Hera. But he's nice and he builds everything for us in Olympus. Oops, look at the time, I have got to go get ready for a wedding!!!

F1-JANE. Oh, who's getting married?

F2-APHRODITE. The sea nymph Thetis is marrying one of the first humans, King Peleus! *(beat)* I think I'll wear white!

*(**APHRODITE** exits.)*

F1-JANE. We'll look for you there.

*(**THOR** [**M2**] enters carrying his hammer.)*

Ladies and Gentlemen: Look, I believe it's Ares, God of War!!!!

M2-THOR. *(caught, lying with thick Norwegian accent)* Jah! Dats Me! I em Ee-rees, Gad uff Var, Jah!

F1-JANE. Hey wait a minute! You're Thor. You're a Norse God! Security! Wow. Can you believe that, Tom?

*(**THOR** looks around and makes a quick escape. **TOM** [**M1**] enters.)*

M1-TOM. Oh that Thor! Sadly, we've just been notified that the real Ares, can't be here right now, he's preparing for the Trojan War.

F1-JANE. That's a shame Tom, but really nice foreshadowing again.

M1-TOM. Thanks. We're not missing much, Jane. Ares is pretty much a mean coward of a deity, who runs away when he gets wounded. He keeps pretty unpleasant company like his sister Discord and her son Strife and the Goddess of War, Enyo.

F1-JANE. Oh, I hate her music! It's so annoying…anya-hoodoo, enya-frodo, whatever…

*(**JANE** [**F1**] exits.)*

M1-TOM. Well, as I said, I'm sure we'll get to see him during the Iliad. Next on our list is the Goddess of the Hearth and symbol of the home. She's a virgin goddess and the sister of Zeus…it's Hestia!!!!

(**HESTIA** *[F2] enters. She wears a crinoline skirt and pearls.)*

Thank you for coming out tonight. Unfortunately, you have NO distinct personality and play NO PART in the myths.

*(***TOM** *gently yet firmly guides her out.* **HESTIA**, *who was clearly looking forward to saying something, leaves with her mouth agape.)*

Wasn't she great?! Finally, rounding out the 12 Great Olympians, he's best known as the Messenger of the Gods. Heeeeerre's HERMES!!!!!

(SFX -rock crowd cheering. **HERMES** *[M3] enters and uses his wand as a mike.* **TOM** *exits.)*

M3-HERMES. Wassup my peeps! Glad to be here tonight! As Messenger of the Gods, I'd like to send some shout-outs for tonight!

I wanna' say "You Go Girl!" to Iris, Goddess of the Rainbow, who is the other messenger of the gods… you have my 'spect, baby girl!

I wanna give "a tip of the winged hat" to Eros, baby B-boy and God of Love!

Three "shouts" to the Three Graces; Splendor, Mirth and Good Cheer! I wanna party with you! And don't forget my nine Muses…your names may be hard but you know you're hardcore awesome!

"What up?!" to my main men Zeus's sidekicks, Themis and Dike. There is no justice like Human or Divine Justice…you know I'm talking about you! And a "wave" to Poseidon's pals Proteus and Triton.

"Wild words" to my son Pan!

Last and definitely not least, to the humans about to be invented I wanna say, "Good luck, you're gonna need it!" And since I've got the mike…

(becoming serious)

The Creation of Mankind

M3-HERMES Now is the time to populate the world with creatures of all shape, kind and manner. The Titans Metheus, come forth and be commanded.

*(***EPIMETHEUS** *[***M1***] and* **PROMETHEUS** *[***M2***] enter. Epimetheus is clearly A.D.D., while Prometheus is obviously level-headed and smart.)*

Epimetheus and Prometheus. You stood by the side of mighty Zeus when he fought Cronus, and for that he is indebted. Now he gives to you this honor. Make mankind.

M2-PROMETHEUS. It shall be.

*(***HERMES** *exits.)*

M1-EPIMETHEUS. So cool. Okay. Make all the creatures great and small. *(pulling out large instruction manual and quickly flipping pages)* This is too long. Too many words…no pictures...

M2-PROMETHEUS. Alright, making the creatures & don't forget mankind.

M1-EPIMETHEUS. *(tosses book)* I got it. Lets give the deer antlers. The bears get fur and claws. The hippo gets two giant white teeth, but only on the bottom of the mouth.

M2-PROMETHEUS. And mankind…

M1-EPIMETHEUS. No wait. I know. The monkeys, will throw poo to defend themselves. The elephant can squirt fire out of its nose…and the mynah bird should have laser eyes that shoot lasers!

M2-PROMETHEUS. Impressive. Poo, fire, lasers. And what have you left for man? We're supposed to make the humans. You've given all the good stuff to the creatures.

M1-EPIMETHEUS. Crap. I forgot to save anything cool for the humans. What do I do now? You gotta help me!

M2-PROMETHEUS. Alright calm down. Let me see what we've got.

M1-EPIMETHEUS. Thanks. Great. Hey man! Here man! Stay! Sit! I said stay! Good man. Good man!

*(***MAN** *[M3] enters like a monkey, then squats.)*

M2-PROMETHEUS. That's it? He has nothing to protect himself. He'll never be able to master the beasts.

M1-EPIMETHEUS. Zeus is gonna' be pissed.

M2-PROMETHEUS. Wait a second. What if we make him more in Zeus's image. More like him.

*(***EPIMETHEUS** *poses and* **PROMETHEUS** *then shapes* **MAN** *upright. They both look at him for a second and groan in disappointment.)*

M1-EPIMETHEUS. That's the best you can do?

M2-PROMETHEUS. Give me a minute I'm thinking!

M1-EPIMETHEUS. Well think faster!

M2-PROMETHEUS. HEY! It wasn't me who gave the mynah bird laser eyes!

M1-EPIMETHEUS. Okay fine! So we give the laser eyes to man!

M2-PROMETHEUS. It's not as easy as that Epi! Listen, if you give man lasers or claws or whatever, he'll just hurt himself. Man is a stupid, stupid creature. What would be really smart is to make him...smart.

M1-EPIMETHEUS. Okay. How do we do that?

M2-PROMETHEUS. I shall steal fire and give it to man.

(He takes a lighter out and gives it to **MAN** *who gleefully plays with it. Dramatically to audience.)*

And now upright, though man may be feeble and weak and short-lived, he now has flaming fire, and from that he shall learn many crafts.

M1-EPIMETHEUS. Who are you talking to???

M2-PROMETHEUS. Never mind…just…go get Zeus and tell him we're ready.

*(**EPIMETHEUS** quick changes to **ZEUS** [**M1**].)*

Mighty Zeus, I present you with man.

(SFX – drum roll.)

M3-MAN. *(weakly)* Ta-da.

M1-ZEUS. That's it? Where's the claws, the laser beams, the poo?

M2-PROMETHEUS. He has not need for those, for man has been made in your image and all fear and respect you, Lord of the Sky.

M1-ZEUS. My image, huh…okay…Wait! You didn't give him my lightning bolts did you?

M2-PROMETHEUS. Of course not. I have only given him fire.

M1-ZEUS. Oh, that's okay if it's just…what?!!! FIRE! Are you crazy? Now he's going to learn! Now we have to keep an eye on him forever. *(actor, referring to himself)* Why can't you be more like Epimetheus, so handsome and playful and funny and…

M2-PROMETHEUS. *(scrambling)* This is just the prototype Zeus. He is new and shiny and shall live without sorrow of heart, far from toil. He shall worship you and we shall call this the Golden Race of Man.

M1-ZEUS. *(beat)* I don't like it.

M2-PROMETHEUS. Okay…when the Golden Boys are gone, we shall make a Silver Race…like the Golds, just not as smart.

M1-ZEUS. They're hardly Ivy League material now. If they're any dimmer they'll injure themselves and each other.

M2-PROMETHEUS. Well we can make him any way you like…

M1-ZEUS. I dunno. This mankind thing sounds like a lot of work on my part. Let's just smite them before this goes too far.

*(**MAN** hides behind **PROMETHEUS** who tries to protect him.)*

M2-PROMETHEUS. No!…no no no. Let me keep him. I'll take care of him I promise! Tell you what…just let them run wild for awhile, then *YOU* can zap 'em when it's all done. Fun, right? Right?

M1-ZEUS. So they run themselves for a while and then I get to smite them.

M2-PROMETHEUS. *(claps calling in* **CAROL***)* Right! And look over here. They've even prepared sacrifice to you already. They know You're the Man!

M1-ZEUS. I'm "The God!"

*(***CAROL** *[***F1***] enters with two plates, one covered with burlap, the other with gold satin. She displays them like a game show.)*

M2-PROMETHEUS. Of course. So which sacrifice do you want?

M1-ZEUS. *(to audience)* Uhm…I don't know. What should I do??? The gold looks good…but it could be a zonk! Maybe it's the burlap…I just don't know…uhm, I want you to uncover them.

M2-PROMETHEUS. Oh. Okay. As you can see, one is glistening and tasty looking and one is not as appealing. *(beat)* 99 minute show, Zeus. Let's go.

M1-ZEUS. I want the tasty looking one. Final answer.

M2-PROMETHEUS. Oh…Zeus, I'm sorry, you chose the bones and shining fat.

(SFX: wah wah wah. **CAROL** *exits on Zeus' line.)*

That leaves the meat and leather for mankind.

M1-ZEUS. Argh!!! Prometheus!!! You tricked me! You are in big trouble mister. However, I've given my word and I'll stick to it. Prometheus! You did a bang up job with man, so I'm going to give you a brand new home up high on the Caucasus, a high jagged rock where you shall be bound by adamantine chains that none can break. And an eagle will come to visit you, and feast on your liver every day. All because...You pissed me off!

And Man! Before I go, I want to give you a little gift from all the Gods…in fact that is her name, meaning "the gift of all." You pronounce it Pandora.

*(***PANDORA*** [***F2***] enters adorable and attractive.* ***MAN*** *is obviously infatuated with her instantly.)*

M2-PROMETHEUS. Oh NO!

M1-ZEUS. Oh YES! Man shall have his mate. She is of the same material and equal in most ways. She is brave and careless; angry and gracious; foolish and smarter than man by just a hair. Oh, and curious! So curious! She hungers for knowledge and will ask man questions... LOTS AND LOTS of questions. And when a man has all he needs, for he is simple and needs only food, sleep and a mate, she will wonder why? Why is that all he needs? Why doesn't he need more? Why doesn't he want more? If he had more, would he want it? Would he not want it? Why would he want it or not want it? Why? Why?

M2-PROMETHEUS. Man won't stand for it.

M1-ZEUS. Yes he will, for you have made him in my image... standing. Oh, I almost forgot. A present for Pandora. Carol!

*(***CAROL*** [***F1***] brings out a small closed trunk and key, hands it to* ***ZEUS****, and exits.)*

Pandora, go and live with man. Be happy, have fun. Here is a gift for you. The only thing is you can NEVER open this box. Here's the key. Remember...NEVER open the box. Now get out of here you crazy kids! That's all the time we have folks!!! Goodnight!!!!

Pandora

*(***ZEUS*** leads* **PROMETHEUS** *off, leaving* **PANDORA** *and* **MAN** *on stage.* **MAN** *takes a seat and starts to read the paper.* **PANDORA** *continues to ponder the box.)*

M3-MAN. *(reading)* Sweetheart, look at this. Another mynah bird related death.

F2-PANDORA. I wonder what's in the box? Don't you wonder what's in there?

M3-MAN. Nope. Zeus said don't open it. I believe him.

F2-PANDORA. Yeah, but what if it's something nice, like a bed ruffle?

M3-MAN. Why would Zeus tell you to never open a box that has a bed ruffle? Do we even need a bed ruffle?

F2-PANDORA. Of course we need a bed ruffle. You're so silly!!!! How could we live without a bed ruffle? *(***MAN*** stares agape in wonder.)* Ooooh, what if it's a baby!

M3-MAN. Why would he put a baby in a box?

F2-PANDORA. Maybe that's where all the babies are going to come from? Did you ever stop and think about that?

M3-MAN. *(***MAN*** stares agape in wonder.)* Well, yes I have. You know, I am made in Zeus' image. I have an idea where all the babies are going to come from.

(She looks curious, so he whispers to her with some odd hand gestures NOT actually depicting how babies are made. She is clearly fascinated, amused and disgusted at his description. Finally she just laughs out loud.)

F2-PANDORA. You've GOT to be KIDDING.

*(***MAN*** goes back to his paper.)*

(beat) What do you think is in the box?

M3-MAN. I don't know.

F2-PANDORA. Aren't you even curious?

M3-MAN. Nope.

F2-PANDORA. Why not?

M3-MAN. Why should I be? Zeus said never open it.

F2-PANDORA. That means he *wants* me to open it.

M3-MAN. What are you talking about, he said *never* open it.

F2-PANDORA. Right…but he knows what's in the box. If he really didn't want me to open it, he wouldn't have given it to me.

M3-MAN. No, if he didn't want you to open it he would have said, *NEVER* open it.

F2-PANDORA. Then why did he give me the key?

M3-MAN. Just because someone gives you a key doesn't mean they want you to use it.

F2-PANDORA. Name one time you give someone a key if you don't want them to use it.

M3-MAN. Okay, what if I give a house key to Frank…

F2-PANDORA. Who's Frank?

M3-MAN. He's our neighbor.

F2-PANDORA. When did we get a neighbor?

M3-MAN. It doesn't matter. Just pretend, we have a neighbor named Frank and we give him our house key. It doesn't mean we want him to use it. We say *NEVER* use our house key, just keep it in case we lose our own so we can use it later. That's why Zeus gave the key to you. So he can use it himself later.

F2-PANDORA. *(a little pouty)* Oh. *(beat)* How do we know Frank didn't use our key?

M3-MAN. Because we told him NEVER use the key.

F2-PANDORA. But can we trust Frank?

M3-MAN. Forget Frank! How can I explain this? Some things just go together. It's like a pillow sham and a bed ruffle. They go together but you don't use them.

F2-PANDORA. You're supposed to use them.

M3-MAN. Fine. We'll use a pillow sham and a bed ruffle.

F2-PANDORA. So I should open the box.

M3-MAN. Zeus said NEVER open the box.

F2-PANDORA. Right, but he didn't say anything about the key. *(**MAN** stares agape in wonder)* He clearly wants me to use the key or he would have said NEVER use the key.

M3-MAN. He said **NEVER** open the box.

F2-PANDORA. But he didn't say **NEVER** use the key, did he?? Did HE???

M3-MAN. I guess not.

F2-PANDORA. Good. You open it.

M3-MAN. No way!

F2-PANDORA. Please!

M3-MAN. Not a chance!

F2-PANDORA. Pretty please!

M3-MAN. No.

F2-PANDORA. Well, why not?!

M3-MAN. Because Zeus said.

F2-PANDORA. Zeus said! Zeus said!

M3-MAN. You'd better stop. Seriously, you're going to be sorry.

F2-PANDORA. Fine. I'll do it myself.

M3-MAN. Don't.

F2-PANDORA. It's my box. And my key.

M3-MAN. Pandora. Listen to me. I love you. So seriously, this is the last time I'm going to say this, because I don't want to say "I told you so," …believe me when I say this: ***DON'T OPEN THE BOX.***

(She smiles sweetly and gives man a sweet kiss.)

F2-PANDORA. You said you love me!

(She walks happily to the box, unlocks it and opens it. Lights and SFX: Dark scary ominous loud shrieking woeful sound and lights scaring both **MAN** *and* **PANDORA**. *She quickly closes the box and the noise stops while the lights change to dim. Beat. She instantly turns mad at* **MAN** *before he even opens his mouth to say…)*

M3-MAN. I told you…

F2-PANDORA. Don't You Dare! This is all your fault!

M3-MAN. My fault? How is this my fault?!

F2-PANDORA. If you had just told me to ***NEVER*** open the box…

*(***PANDORA** *exits, quick change to Persephone.* **MAN** *stopped in his tracks.)*

M1-ZEUS VOICE OFFSTAGE. Man?!?!? What did you do?!!!!!!!

(A beat. **MAN** *exits saying…)*

M3-MAN. Son of a…

The Earth Goddess – Demeter and Persephone

*(**DEMETER** [**F1**] enters.)*

F1-DEMETER. *(to audience)* And now the story of Demeter and Persephone. *(happily calling offstage)* Persephone, my sweet! Come here darling.

*(**PERSEPHONE** [**F2**] runs in giggling.)*

F2-PERSEPHONE. Yes Mother! Mother, I love the Earth you have made for mankind. The land is lush and so wondrously lovely.

F1-DEMETER. Thank you my darling. Have a good time but do not wander too far.

*(**DEMETER** exits.)*

F2-PERSEPHONE. I shall collect a bouquet of the prettiest flowers there are, to give to my mother.

*(**PERSEPHONE** collects flowers. She moves near one side of the stage and **HADES'** Helmet on a Stick appears from the wings. She does not see him, of course.)*

M2-HADES' VOICE FROM OFFSTAGE. Ah this beauty. I, Hades, King of the Underworld, I have never seen such beauty before.

(dialogue accelerates and overlaps)

F2-PERSEPHONE. Ah, this beauty I have never seen before. Such a display.

M2-HADES VOICE FROM OFFSTAGE. Such a radiant display. I must have her for my own.

F2-PERSEPHONE. Oh look at this wondrous flower. What?? A chasm in the earth???

*(**SFX** - rumbling earth)*

*(She screams and mimes falling. The helmet disappears as **HADES** steps onstage driving two black hobby horses.)*

M2-HADES. It is I, Hades, full of dark splendor, beautiful and majestic and terrible.

F2-PERSEPHONE. Oh, hell.

M2-HADES. Exactly

(They exit. **DEMETER** *re-enters.* **SKY** *[M1] and* **WIND** *[M3] enter.)*

F1-DEMETER. Persephone?! Where are you my daughter? Sky?

M1-SKY. Can't help you, sorry.

F1-DEMETER. Wind?!?

M3-WIND. No English.

*(**APOLLO** [M2] enters.)*

F1-DEMETER. Can no one help me? Good sun, mighty Apollo. Where is my daughter?

M2-APOLLO. Demeter, Goddess of the Corn, Mother of Persephone and all around sweetheart. Hades took her to be his queen.

*(**APOLLO** exits, leaving her to her woe.)*

F1-DEMETER. Oh cruel fate! My most beautiful creation gone to the dark underworld! I am sad! I shall withhold my gifts from this Earth until I get my daughter back. No warmth shall I bring. No seed shall sprout. There shall be no harvest to reap.

(Cast switches as appropriate.)

M3-MAN. Great Goddess! We have built you a temple and yet you forsake us! Zeus! Our father! Help Us! We are certain to die of famine and this is SO not our fault!

M1-ZEUS. *(exasperated)* Here we go! I have to take care of Man! Fine. Hermes!

M3-HERMES. Yo!

M1-ZEUS. Go tell Hades he has to give Persephone back.

*(**PERSEPHONE & HADES** re-enter. She is eating pomegranate seeds.)*

M3-HERMES. Right. Hades! She must go back or man shall die.

M2-HADES. What?!!! Aww C'mon!!!

M3-HERMES. Hey, Zeus says. That's how I roll.

M2-HADES. Persephone. Your beauty is unmatched and I love you. Be kind, for I am King of the Underworld and if you stay you shall be my Queen.

F2-PERSEPHONE. Look. You're a nice God. Really nice but, *(packing and moving for a quick exit)* well…it's not you, it's me. Really! And you know my mom, she wanted a big wedding with all the Gods there. You amd I just sort of eloped. Actually you kind of kidnapped me. Anyway, I really do think you're sweet… *(aside to* **HERMES***)* **Start the chariot**. *(back to* **HADES***)* I'll call you, okay?

M2-HADES. Whatever.

M3-HERMES. Here she is! Home again!

F2-PERSEPHONE. Momma!

F1-DEMETER. Persy! I missed you so much!

M3-MAN. Still dying of hunger here!

F1-DEMETER. Oh right! Sorry! My bad! Reap! Harvest! Eat! How about you sweetheart? Are you hungry?

F2-PERSEPHONE. No, I just ate some pomegranate seeds before I left the underworld.

M3-HERMES. Whoa, whoa whoa…Hold on there, Princess. The Fates say that once you have eaten in the underworld you cannot leave.

F1 & F2-DEMETER & PERSEPHONE. What?!!!

M3-HERMES. Hey, the Fates say. That's how I roll.

M2-HADES. Yeah!

F2-PERSEPHONE. Zeus?!!! I didn't eat a whole pomegranate, just a few seeds.

M1-ZEUS. Then you shall go back to be the Queen with Hades for one third of the year.

M2-HADES. YES!!!! She's all 1/3rd mine!

F1-DEMETER. Then while Persephone lives here with me it shall be beautiful and bounteous, and when she must go my heart shall turn cold and the land shall be barren and that time shall be called Winter.

(All exiting except **ZEUS***.)*

M3-MAN. Oh nice. *That's* fair!

M1-ZEUS. Quit your whining already!

The Earth God – Dionysus

M1-ZEUS. Hello! What's this??? A beautiful princess of Thebes by the name of Semele. So beautiful and truly a delight to the eyes. Semele, I'm King of the Gods. I love you!

*(**ZEUS** walks to a woman in the audience. He will flirt and play with the audience woman and obviously lie to **HERA**, who is offstage to begin.)*

M2-HERA OFFSTAGE. Sweetheart?

M1-ZEUS. Hera?! Crap! Don't worry about her, baby. Here she comes. Act like you don't know me.

*(**ZEUS** talks to the man sitting next to audience woman as **HERA** enters.)*

M2-HERA. Zeus. Do you know where I put my nice sandals? *(beat)* What are you doing?

M1-ZEUS. Nothing! I'm, uh…just talking with a man. *(points with lightning bolts so **HERA** knows which audience member)* This man here and NOT Semele, this attractive woman beside him.

M2-HERA. *(suspiciously)* Really. What were you talking about, hmmm?

M1-ZEUS. Oh you know. Ah, building temples and herding goats…the normal God to mortal stuff. Bow mortal! *(gets audience man to bow)* Your sandals are under the thing…near the stuff …by the plant.

*(**HERA** stares at **ZEUS** and woman and man. Then turns and leaves abruptly.)*

Whew, that was close. Semele, my sweet. Did she scare you?

*(**HERA** enters and stands directly in front of audience woman. As **ZEUS** exits, he gestures to audience woman to keep cool.)*

M2-HERA. I can't find them. Will you get them for me? I'll wait here for you. *(turns to make him leave)* You think

I don't know what's going on. He'll promise you the moon, but if you want his love make him prove it. Make him swear by the River Styx, the Oath that can never be broken, to give you whatever you want, and then ask to see the real him, in all his Godlike glory. You'd better write it down to remember. Here, let me help.

*(**HERA** hands dialogue to audience woman, turns to leave and walks directly out, never stopping as **ZEUS** returns with sandals which she grabs from him as she passes. **ZEUS** goes directly to woman, totally acting up the love.)*

M1-ZEUS. Don't worry, she's gone now baby. Let's just be together, you and me. You want the moon…you've got it. Anything you want, you name it.

(This is the prompt to get the audience woman to read:)

AUDIENCE WOMAN. If you love me, then swear by the Styx you'll give me anything I want.

M1-ZEUS. By the Styx…sure. *(a capella)* LAAAAAA-DDDYYYYY! When I'm with you…

AUDIENCE WOMAN. By the River Styx.

M1-ZEUS. Oh, the RIVER Styx. I swear baby, by the River Styx, anything you want.

AUDIENCE WOMAN. Show me yourself in all your Godlike glory.

M1-ZEUS. Aww! Hera put you up to this, didn't she? Fine! I swore by the River Styx. Come with me…

*(**ZEUS** leads her to the wings, and speaks to her and the audience. She is just offstage being dressed.)*

I will show you and then sadly you shall perish for no mortal can see the brilliant wonder that is me. You will flail about and shriek, cry and moan, pull out your hair and scream as you die an agonizing death. And you will do it in an entertaining and fully committed manner, that may even be mentioned in the review.

(The remainder of the cast rushes onstage and sits down.)

ALL RANDOMLY. She's going to do the death scene, cool. This is the most exciting part of the show. Awesome! Death scene! Move over I want to see this.

M1-ZEUS. And now my true glory.

(Blackout. Drum roll. **ZEUS** *shines flashlight on his own face and* **CAST** *says "Ooooh." Lights up.)*

And now Semele...*(directing)* in an energetic, committed and entertaining manner ...you will flail about and shriek *(waits for her)*, cry and moan *(again)*, pull out your hair *(hopefully she will pull off the wig)*, and scream as you die an agonizing death *(wait)*.

(As woman dies, the cast leap to their feet in applause and surround her, taking her props. The men will escort audience woman back to her seat then stand onstage, and the women will take the baby and exit when Zeus gives it to them.)

Sad Semele. Fair spirits, guide her soul back to her seat to thunderous applause from the audience.

Alas, I have saved the child she carried. I give it to you, the nymphs of Nysa. He is born of the burning heat of my glory and nursed by the rain of your land to keep him alive, just like the grapes are.

As the child grows, he shall meet the jovial, fat, drunken, donkey-riding Silenus, who shall teach him the craft and art of the drink and this child shall grow to be Dionysus, The God of Wine.

He will share his gifts with man who will, unfortunately, have no self control. They will drink to excess and grow angry and belligerent.

M2-DRUNKEN MAN. What are you looking at?

M3-DRUNKEN MAN. Well what are you looking at?

(Beat. They struggle.)

M1-ZEUS. Others will turn happy and generous.

M3-DRUNKEN MAN. I love you, man!

M2-DRUNKEN MAN. You're my best friend! Nothing can come between us!

(Beat. Quick embrace.)

M1-ZEUS. And it shall not just be man. Woman shall love the vine as well.

(**F1 & F2** *stagger in laughing like they've been at a bar for too long for girls night out. The two pairs regard each other.)*

M3-DRUNKEN MAN. Look at the skanks.

F1-DRUNKEN WOMAN. Check out the dorks.

(Beat. Quick make out pairings.)

M1-ZEUS. And in this way, much of the earth was populated. *(beat)* Now, to learn more, here is a Greek chorus.

(They all become a Greek chorus.)

ALL AS GREEK CHORUS. This is the story of Dionysus and the King of Thebes.

We are the Maenads, the madwomen! We worship Dionysus in the wild. We follow him everywhere, frenzied with wine, dancing and singing. We are the madwomen! *(They do so, for a circuit around the stage.)*

We have followed Dionysus to the city Thebes, where his mother Semele *(gesture to woman from audience)* was overacting when she died.

King Pentheus of Thebes does not like Dionysus or the crazed dancing and singing of the madwomen! *(They do another circuit.)*

And so he ordered the guards to seize us! *(they all attempt to seize each other for a moment)*

M2-THESPIS. And now I, Thespis, the first man to step out of the Greek chorus…

ALL THE REST. That's history, not Mythology!

M2-THESPIS. …will play the part of the great old blind prophet Tiresias as he tries to warn King Pentheus.

"Oh Pentheus, King of Thebes, hear my solemn warning. The man you reject is a new god."

2 OF CHORUS AS PENTHEUS/You're no God!

3 OF CHORUS AS DIONYSUS/Yes I am.

2 OF CHORUS AS PENTHEUS/No you're not!

3 OF CHORUS AS DIONYSUS/Your mother believes me.

2 OF CHORUS AS PENTHEUS/I'm going to chase you!

3 OF CHORUS AS DIONYSUS/I tried to warn you.

2 OF CHORUS AS PENTHEUS/AAAAUUUUGGGHHHHH!

GREEK CHORUS. We saw Pentheus and thought he was a wild beast and pounced upon him and tore him limb from limb, because we are the madwomen! *(They pounce upon themselves and end in a pile.)*

(SFX – school bell. Actors arrange themselves as kindergarten class.)

The Love Stories, Pt. 1

F1-MS. HENDERSON. So class, did you finish your homework on Greek Love stories?

F2-STUDENT. They were so sad. Ms. Henderson? Do all love stories end in tragedy?

F1-MS. HENDERSON. Yes, Amy. Yes they do.

M1-STUDENT. Well, my mom says that not every love story is a tragedy and she says you're twisted because Principal Thomas dumped you.

F1-MS. HENDERSON. First of all, I dumped *him.* Secondly, your mother is a drunk with bad teeth. *All* Greek Love stories are tragic. Apollo and Daphne, Narcissus and Echo, Zeus and Callisto, Zeus and Leto, Brad and Jennifer *[or insert first names of current topical celebrity couple breakup here]* ...TRAGIC!

F2-STUDENT. I don't care what you say! I think it would be cool to have a God like Zeus love me!

F1-MS. HENDERSON. A God like Zeus...who's MARRIED TO HERA and tries to have an affair with Io – but when Hera catches on, Zeus turns Io into a white heifer but Hera still blames poor IO for the whole mess and sends gadflies to sting her and gossips about her to the PTA until she goes insane. So poor Io wanders for years and ends up in another school until one day Zeus finally shows his face and turns her mortal again. That Zeus??? Is that the god you're talking about?!?!?!?!?!?!?!!!!!!!!

(A beat, then all the children start to cry. **PRINCIPAL THOMAS** *[M2] enters.)*

M2-PRINCIPAL THOMAS. Hey! What's going on in here?

F1-MS. HENDERSON. Zeus...uhh...I mean Principal Thomas.

M3-STUDENT. Ms. Henderson was telling us love stories!!!!!

M2-PRINCIPAL THOMAS. Really. Did she tell you about Eros and Psyche?

STUDENTS. *(afraid)* Nooooo!

M2-PRINCIPAL THOMAS. Psyche was the most beautiful woman on earth and Eros fell instantly in love with Psyche, even though he told her right up front that he was in a relationship.

Psyche, who was desperate for love, went along willingly…her own choice…and the winds took her to a beautiful place where she had anything she wanted.

F1-MS. HENDERSON. But she couldn't see her lover. It was all just words!

M2-PRINCIPAL THOMAS. But she knew it was true love… Unfortunately her sisters showed up. They were jealous, so they convinced Psyche to hide a lamp near her bed so she could see her husband, even though the voice (who loved her) warned her NOT to LISTEN to her SISTERS.

That night Psyche lit the lantern and saw her husband, who was EROS, The God of Love. In her shock, Psyche spilled the lantern and burned Eros very badly, and because Love can't live where there is no trust, he ran away.

F1-MS. HENDERSON. Psyche realized her mistake.

M2-PRINCIPAL THOMAS. It took Eros some time to heal, but now Eros and Psyche…Heart and Mind…Love and the Soul…

F2-STUDENT. Live happily ever after?

(**PRINCIPAL THOMAS** *kisses* **MS. HENDERSON**. *Students cheer!!!)*

M1-STUDENT. And now it's time for the wedding of King Peleus and the sea-nymph Thetis!

ALL. Hooray!

(They all scatter leaving **ZEUS** *[***M1***] and* **M3** *onstage.)*

The Wedding that started it all.

M3-NARRATOR. It was a grand celebration of the noteworthy union of the mortal King Peleus and the Sea-Goddess Thetis. Everyone was invited except the Goddess of Discord, who showed up anyway, with a terrible wedding gift.

M3-ERIS. This ought to stir things up!

(Winds up and pitches golden apple to **ZEUS**. **GODDESSES** *will strike fighting poses on dialogue as they enter.)*

M1-ZEUS. *(reading)* "For the Fairest."

M2- HERA. Surely, it must be for me, Hera!

F1- ATHENA. Obviously, it's for me, Athena!

F2-APHRODITE. Sillies! You're both wrong. It's gotta be for me, Aphrodite!

(Quick bicker, then turn to **ZEUS***.)*

M2-HERA. Oh wise Zeus, you must decide this matter. Which of us is the fairest?

M1-ZEUS. I'm not touching that one with a ten foot lightning bolt. We'll let a mortal decide, like…Paris, the shepherd! Catch!

*(***ZEUS** *tosses the apple to* **PARIS** *[M3].* **GODDESSES** *rush him.)*

M2-HERA. I'll give you power! *(showing crown)*

F1-ATHENA. I'll give you wisdom. *(showing mortarboard)*

F2-APHRODITE. I'll give you the most beautiful woman in the world! *(shows centerfold)*

M3-PARIS. Wow! Queen Helen of Sparta! We have a winner! Aphrodite! Sparta, here I come!

*(***PARIS** *crosses to* **HELEN** *[F2].* **ZEUS** *becomes* **MENELAOS***.)*

F2-HELEN. Welcome to Sparta. I'm Queen Helen and this is my husband Menelaos. Honey, we have company!

M1-MENELAOS. Be right there! *(into cell phone)* …and then

Diogenes says, "Actually, I was just looking for my car keys."

F2-HELEN. So, what brings you to Sparta?

M3-PARIS. Funny you should ask. Beautiful Queen Helen, have you ever dreamed of a better life than this?

F2-HELEN. I have the perfect life; beloved by my people, adored by my husband, my every need attended to and I have more wealth than anyone could imagine.

M3-PARIS. *(shrugs)* Well, Aphrodite promised...

*(***PARIS** *takes* **HELEN** *away.)*

M1-MENELAOS. I'll call you back. I gotta call my brother. Agamemnon!

*(***AGAMEMNON** *[***M3***] enters w/ sword at the ready.)*

M3-AGAMEMNON. I'm here, Brother! What danger threatens our land?

M1-MENELAOS. Paris just stole Helen and took her to Troy!

M3-AGAMEMNON. The Trojans, hm? Well, we could try diplomacy to get her back, but...let's just go to war! You round up the army. I'll get our two greatest warriors, Brave Odysseus and Mighty Achilles.

*(***AGAMEMNON** *exits.* **MENELAOS** *becomes* **ACHILLES** *joining entering* **ODYSSEUS** *[***M2***].)*

M1-ACHILLES. ...so I said, "Sorry, Oedipus. I don't think Hallmark even *makes* a card for that!" Oh look, an Oracle.

*(***ORACLE** *[***F1***] enters. SFX – Oracle music)*

F1-ORACLE. Beware Warriors!

If you go to war, then YOU, Odysseus, shall not return home for 20 years!

...and YOU, Achilles shall die young! *(pointing to various people in the audience)*

...and YOU! You shall find true love, but it will cost you every bit of your self-esteem and most of your tax refund!

...and YOU! You shall successfully steal cable but lose your remote control!

...and YOU! You will order Diet Coke at McDonald's, but will receive Regular Coke!

M1-ACHILLES. That's enough!

F1-ORACLE. ...and *you* will be singled out as the weak spot in the show.

*(**ORACLE** exits. **AGAMEMNON** [**M3**] enters.)*

M2-ODYSSEUS. Oh man! It's Agamemnon. He's gonna try to get us to go to war! Hide!

*(**ACHILLES** hides but **AGAMEMNON** sees **ODYSSEUS**.)*

M3-AGAMEMNON. Hail Brave Odysseus! We're going to war!

M2-ODYSSEUS. Ah, I'd love too, but, uhm...I'm crazy! Yeah! Woo-hoo! Booga-booga!

M3-AGAMEMNON. Too bad. We're going to go rescue Helen at Troy *(outlines hourglass figure)*

M2-ODYSSEUS. Hubba hubba!

M3-AGAMEMNON. Aha!

*(**AGAMEMNON** grabs **ODYSSEUS**' ear as **ACHILLES** tries to sneak by in a dress and wig.)*

Hail, Achilles!

M1-ACHILLES. My name is...*(bad falsetto)* Achillita. I cannot go to war, hee-hee.

M3-AGAMEMNON. Too bad. We're going to rescue Helen of Troy. *(outline figure)*

M1-ACHILLES. Helen of Troy! Hubba-hubba.

M3-AGAMEMNON. Aha!

M1-ACHILLES. Rats! I'm keeping the dress though!

M3-AGAMEMNON. To the ships! And victory!

(They mime ship activity.)

M1-ACHILLES. The winds keep blowing us back to port! We cannot sail! Why is this Oracle?

*(**ORACLE** re-appears and exits with dialogue.)*

F1-ORACLE. Agamemnon killed Artemis' favorite deer. She will only be appeased by the sacrifice of his daughter Iphigenia.

(They huddle and finally **AGAMEMNON** *gives in.)*

M3-AGAMEMNON. Alright! Oh Iphigenia! Come here sweet-ums. Achilles wants to marry you!

*(***IPHIGENIA** *[***F2***] appears.)*

F2-IPHIGENIA. I'm so happy, daddy!

M3-AGAMEMNON. Yeah. Sorry about this, kitten.

*(***AGAMEMNON** *bops her over the head and throws her overboard. SFX-splash)*

Boy, that's gonna be tough to explain to the wife. But here comes the wind! Troy, here we come!

(Others sail off leaving **M3**. **M2** *divides the stage in half with tape, indicating Trojan and Greek sides of conflict.)*

M3-NARRATOR. And thus begins the Iliad proper, all twenty four books! Time check! Oh! **BOOK ONE!** After nine years of battle in Troy, one night Agamemnon and Achilles captured two beautiful maidens named Chrissyus and Brissyus.

M3-FATHER. My daughter Chrissyus has been captured! Mighty Apollo, I beg you send a plague on those Greek swine!

M2-APOLLO VOICE OFFSTAGE. You got it!

*(***ACHILLES** *[***M1***] and* **ORACLE** *[***F1***] enter and join* **AGAMEMNON** *[***M3***].)*

M1-ACHILLES. Agamemnon, we have another call sick. We're gonna have to call a temp agency to fight this war soon.

M3-AGAMEMNON. Oracle, what is causing this plague?

F1-ORACLE. It's Chrissyus. You have to give her back.

M3-AGAMEMNON. Okay, but I get Achilles girl then.

M1-ACHILLES. Dude! No way!

M3-AGAMEMNON. Yes way! I'm the general. That's it!

*(**AGAMEMNON** and **ORACLE** exit.)*

M1-ACHILLES. This is so embarrassing! Agamemnon just screwed me over! MOM!!

*(**THETIS** [**F2**] appears.)*

F2-THETIS. It is I, Thetis, the Goddess of…

M1-ACHILLES. Yeah, Mom, I know who you are. Listen, Agamemnon just threw me under the bus. I want you to go get Zeus to help the Trojans defeat the Greeks.

F2-THETIS. My son, this is not appropriate behavior for a noble warrior such as yourself.

M1-ACHILLES. MOOOMMMMM!

F2-THETIS. I'll see what I can do.

*(**ACHILLES** becomes **ZEUS**. **THETIS** crosses to **ZEUS**.)*

Zeus, please help my son and punish the Greeks

M1-ZEUS. Okay, I'll help the Trojans, but whatever you do don't let my wife Hera know. She's a big Greek booster.

M2-HERA VOICE OFFSTAGE. What are you doing out there? You better not be helping the Trojans!

*(**THETIS** exits. **AGAMEMNON** [**M3**] enters with **ODYSSEUS** [**M2**].)*

M1-NARRATOR. <u>**BOOK TWO!**</u> True to his word, Zeus sent a dream of false victory to Agamemnon, knowing this would prompt rash action.

M3-AGAMEMNON. Odysseus, I had a dream and I know we're going to win! I'll tell the men they can go home if they want, but I know they'll stay out of loyalty. Gather round men!

(All gather and take a knee.)

Men, this is going to be a tough war. So if any of you want to go home now. You can.

*(**MEN** cheer and start to exit.)*

M2-ODYSSEUS. *(rousing, inspirational speech)* Wait! Stop, all of you! What's wrong with you guys? What happened to the Delta Warriors I used to know? *(mocking the men)* "OOOH, we're scared to go with you Odysseus. We might get hurt!" Well I'm not quitting! Not me! Paris is a Dead Man! Priam, Dead! Nedermeyer, Dead! Hector…

M1-NESTOR. DEAD! It is I, wise old Nestor, and Odysseus is right! Now, we could take the diplomatic way and try to reason with the Trojans…but what this situation calls for, is a long, drawn-out, senseless battle of attrition with staggering losses that neither side can truly win. Who's with me? *(They stand.)* Then let's…DO IT!!!!!

(They scream and run out! **M3** *narrates and becomes* **PARIS**.*)*

M3-NARRATOR. Agamemnon reviewed his troops, calling out all their names and deeds as they prepared for battle, making book two much longer than it needed to be. **<u>BOOK THREE!</u>** The armies faced each other outside the walls of Troy where Paris boldly stepped forward and issued a challenge.

M3-PARIS. I challenge any Greek to fight me one on one!

*(***HECTOR** *[***M2***] enters.* **MENELAOS** *[***M1***] enters.)*

M1-MENELAOS. I, Menelaos, husband of Helen, accept your challenge!

*(***PARIS** *shrieks and runs behind* **HECTOR**.*)*

M3-PARIS. Hector, help me!

M2-HECTOR. Dude, you're disgracing the family!

M3-PARIS. Dude, I…twisted my ankle! Dad!

*(***PRIAM** *[***F2***] enters.)*

F2-PRIAM. What's going on here? What kind of war is this? If somebody doesn't take a poke at somebody soon we're all gonna die of old age!

M1-MENELAOS. I agree with King Priam of Troy! This is duller than long form improv! Here's the deal; We fight, winner gets Helen. War over.

F2-PRIAM. Let's get Ready to Rummmb…

M3-PARIS. That's a copywritten slogan!

F2-PRIAM. Oh right. I meant. Let's get Ready…tooo… RUMMMMBBBA!

*(**PRIAM** exits. **MENELAOS** and **PARIS** rumba to music SFX. **MENELAOS** slaps **PARIS**.)*

M1-MENELAOS. Victory! I'm going to Disneyland!

M2-HECTOR. That won't be created for thousands of years. Use the Greek equivalent.

M1-MENELAOS. Oh, right. I'm going to an orgy! [bathhouse! *(for squeaky clean show.)*]

M3-PARIS. Mighty Aphrodite, I've fallen and I can't get up!

*(**APHRODITE** [F2] enters with a blanket and guides **PARIS** off.)*

F2-APHRODITE. I shall blanket you in a thick mist and deliver you to safety.

*(**M2** crosses and becomes **HERA**. **ATHENA** [F1] enters. **M1** changes in his next 3 lines as appropriate.)*

M1-MENELAOS. Hey, no fair using DEUS EX MACHINA!!!! Unsporting I say!

M1-NARRATOR. **BOOK FOUR!** Zeus makes a proclamation in Olympus.

M1-ZEUS. Alright folks, Menelaos won the duel. War's over. Nothing to see here. Let's move along now…

M2-HERA. Wait a minute! I wanted Troy destroyed! Athena, go restart the war for mama.

*(**PANDAROS** [F2] enters and **ATHENA** crosses to him. **ZEUS** and **HERA** exit. **MENELAOS** [M1] enters when mentioned next.)*

F1-ATHENA. Ooooh, Pandaros, you're a fine Trojan warrior. Look at all these weapons lying around… and all your muscles *(feels arm appreciatively)* just going to waste.

F2-PANDAROS. I work out when I can…

F1-ATHENA. How's a stud like you supposed to make his mark in this world when nothing's happening? Say, why don't you shoot Menelaos? I bet that'd stir things up!

F2-PANDAROS. Gee, we're in a truce…

F1-ATHENA. I just *LOVE* war heroes!

F2-PANDAROS. Okay!

(**PANDAROS** *shoots an arrow which* **ATHENA** *carries and sticks to* **MENELAOS**' *butt.* **AGAMEMNON** *[***M3***] appears instantly.)*

M1-MENELAOS. Ouch!

M3-AGAMEMNON. Treachery! Vile Trojans! The truce is off! Prepare for battle! We shall avenge the death of poor Menelaos!

M1-MENELAOS. *(interspersed)* Uh, Agamemnon, I'm right here. It hurts and all, but I'm okay.

M3-AGAMEMNON. That's right men. Menelaos is gone. But before he left, he said one last thing. *(SFX – rousing college fight song swells)* "When the army's up against it, and the breaks are beating the boys… tell 'em to go out there and win one for Gippocrates!"

(**ATHENA** *and* **AGAMEMNON** *exit.* **MENELAOS** *becomes* **ACHILLES**.*)*

F2-NARRATOR. <u>**BOOK FIVE!**</u> The fighting continued fiercer than ever. Meanwhile, Achilles sat in his tent.

(He does. **DIOMEDES** *[***M3***] enters.)*

Back at the battle, the Greek warrior Diomedes was particularly valiant.

M3-DIOMEDES. Diomedes Rules!

(**PANDAROS** *shoots* **DIOMEDES**.*)*

F2-PANDAROS. …until Pandaros the archer wounded him. Hee hee.

M3-DIOMEDES. Fair Athena! You are the most beautiful of all immortals! Help me!

(**ATHENA** *[***F1***] enters.)*

F1-ATHENA. You are not only brave, Diomedes, but wise. Abracadabra. There. All better.

M3-DIOMEDES. Diomedes Rules Again!

(**DIOMEDES** *kills* **PANDAROS** *who exits.)*

F1-ATHENA. As a little bonus, you are now able to distinguish Gods from mortals; but you must *never* use this power to harm a God.

M3-DIOMEDES. I solemnly swear on my honor as a Greek soldier.

F1-ATHENA. Except for Aphrodite. You can cut that bi-yotch!

(**DIOMEDES** *about to kill a passing* **TROJAN** *[***M2***] but* **APHRODITE** *[***F2***] swoops in and holds her hand up stopping* **DIOMEDES**. **TROJAN** *soldier exits.)*

F2-APHRODITE. Stay your sword mortal! You shall harm no Trojan!

M3-DIOMEDES. *(questioning* **ATHENA** *again)* Which God am I allowed to hurt, again?

F1-ATHENA. Aphrodite.

M3-DIOMEDES. That's what I thought. *(to* **APHRODITE***)* Eat blade bi-yotch!!

(**DIOMEDES** *cuts her hand.* **ACHILLES** *becomes* **ZEUS** *and* **ARES** *[***M2***] enters.)*

F2-APHRODITE. Daddy! Diomedes cut my hand! That is so not FAIR!

M1-ZEUS. It's a war for crying out loud! What did you expect?!

M3-ARES. Yeah! It's no place for a woman. Why don't you cast a spell on a shepherd or something?

F2-APHRODITE. Oh SHUT UP ARES! Like you've done anything so far! I don't see you down there!

M3-ARES. Yeah… I guess it's time the Big Dog jumped into this sissy-boy slap fight.

F2-NARRATOR. Meanwhile, Achilles sat in his tent.

(**ZEUS** *becomes* **ACHILLES** *and then switches back.)*

Back at the battle, Athena went to the aid of the Greeks and Diomedes.

F1-ATHENA. Fear no God, Mortal. Especially Ares!

M3-DIOMEDES. Cool. *(slashes* **ARES** *belly)* Diomedes Rules!

M3-ARES. No fair! I'm telling Zeus!

(All run to **ZEUS** *complaining at once.)*

M1-ZEUS. Alright! Enough! Ares, chill out, you're a God, your belly will heal. And Ladies, that's it. No more Gods fighting on either side. I mean it this time.

*(***ZEUS** *and* **ARES** *exit.* **ATHENA** *becomes* **NARRATOR**. **APHRODITE** *becomes* **GLAUKOS**.*)*

F1-NARRATOR. With the Gods sitting out, **BOOK SIX!** Diomedes and Glaukos approach across the battlefield during the truce.

M3-DIOMEDES. Man, this is boring.

F2-GLAUKOS. Yeah. *(beat)* Wanna duel to the death?

M3-DIOMEDES. Sounds good. Let me just get my pre-duel mojo going here. Oh noble ancestors, grant me strength in battle. Let me be brave like my father Radius of Diameter…and my grandfather Duodenum of Oblongata…

F2-GLAUKOS. Wait a sec…your grandfather was from Oblongata? So was mine! His name was Stigmatus.

M3-DIOMEDES. My grandfather's best friend was Stigmatus! Wow! Small world, huh?

F2-GLAUKOS. No kidding! Well, this is awkward. Uhm…I won't kill you. Okay?

M3-DIOMEDES. Right. Me either. I guess we should exchange armor, you know, as a gesture of goodwill.

*(***DIOMEDES** *trades his lousy armor for* **GLAUKOS**' *nice armor. As they exit…)*

F2-GLAUKOS. Wow, I got screwed on that one.

F1-NARRATOR. Meanwhile, Hector was back in Troy where he finds Paris relaxing with Helen.

*(**DIOMEDES** and **GLAUKOS** become **PARIS** and **HELEN** respectively. They sit spooning as **HECTOR** [**M2**] enters.)*

M2-HECTOR. You little sneak! There's a war going on!

M3-PARIS. Then what are you doing here?

M2-HECTOR. Well, actually, there's a kind of truce on right now. But it's going to end soon! You know, it might be nice, for the sake of all the guys DYING out there, if you just made an appearance. Don't you think?

M3-PARIS. You're right. I'll go get my battle gear.

*(**PARIS** exits.)*

F2-HELEN. *(inviting **HECTOR**, patting seat abandoned by **PARIS**)* Why don't you sit a while?

M2-HECTOR. *(pityingly)* You never stop, do you? *(looks, considers, then…)* I gotta go see my wife, Andromache.

*(**NARRATOR** [**F1**] becomes **ANDROMACHE**. She crosses to **HECTOR**. **HELEN** exits.)*

F1-ANDROMACHE. Oh, Hector! Can't you just stop fighting? You are all the family I have left! The Greeks killed all my brothers… and my uncles… and my cousins too… And some second cousin-in-law I didn't even know I had… And they even killed that guy that kind of looked like me so everyone thought we were related, but we weren't, although I always wondered because there was that time my father went away on business…

M2-HECTOR. *(pressing finger to her lips)* Shhh, my love. I hear the fear in your voice, but I am a proud warrior of Troy and we are the bravest, fiercest, mightiest warriors in the world!

*(**PARIS** enters askew.)*

M3-PARIS. I'm ready!

M2-HECTOR. *(beat)* Your armor's on backwards.

*(**PARIS** exits. **HECTOR** and **ANDROMACHE** become **APOLLO** and **ATHENA**.)*

M2-NARRATOR. <u>**BOOK SEVEN!**</u> Apollo and Athena looked down on the battle that waged back and forth.

M2-APOLLO. They've been at it so long. They could really use a break.

F1-ATHENA. I know! We'll arrange a duel between a single great warrior from each side.

M2-APOLLO. Didn't Dad tell us to stay out of this?

F1-ATHENA. Oh, don't worry about him. MORTALS!!! Pick a champ and send him out for a duel!

(**ATHENA** *exits.* **APOLLO** *becomes* **NARRATOR**. **AGAMEMNON** *[M3] and* **MENELAOS** *[M1] enter.)*

M2-NARRATOR. First, Agamemnon and Menelaos pondered who to send.

M3-AGAMEMNON. Well, we could send Achilles *(shouting off)* IF HE WEREN'T SITTING IN HIS TENT POUTING LIKE A BABY!!!!

M1-MENELAOS. Let's send Ajax. He's strong and brave. And clean, too.

(**MENELAOS** *exits.* **AGAMEMNON** *becomes* **TROJAN LACKEY**. **PRIAM** *[F2] enters.)*

M2-NARRATOR. Meanwhile King Priam was selecting a Trojan champion.

F2-PRIAM. I'd like to give Hector a break. Who should we send? Let's send Pandaros.

M3-TROJAN LACKEY. Diomedes killed him in book five, remember?

M3-DIOMEDES. *(sidestep/remove helmet/then back to* **LACKEY***)* DIOMEDES RULES!

F2-PRIAM. Right. How about Paris?

M3-LACKEY. He hides whenever there's a fight.

F2-PRIAM. Ouch. Okay, Glaukos.

M3-LACKEY. He gave away his armor for a pair of shoulder pads and a rubber band.

F2-PRIAM. Hector! You're Up!

(**PRIAM** *and* **LACKEY** *exit.* **HECTOR** *and* **AJAX** *enter.)*

M1-AJAX. Hello. I'm Ajax. I'll be your opponent today.

M2-HECTOR. Nice to meet you. I'm Hector. Shall we?

(Nod. Battle slap fight.)

M1-AJAX. I shall never quit until the ground runs red with your blood, Trojan dog!

M2-HECTOR. As long as there is breath in my body, I will attack you until you lie dead!

(Lights dim.)

Ooooh. It's getting dark.

M1-AJAX. We'd better stop. Nice fight.

M2-HECTOR. You too. How's ten o'clock tomorrow?

M1-AJAX. Sounds good.

*(**AJAX** exits. **ANTENOR** [**F1**] enters laden with plans. He whispers in **HECTOR**'s ear. **PARIS** [**M3**] enters.)*

M2-HECTOR. Listen up everyone. Our master of strategy, Antenor here, has been working day and night. He's calculated every possible angle and scenario and has come up with a plan to ensure a Trojan victory.

F1-ANTENOR. *(clears throat)* Give Helen Back.

M3-PARIS. Wait a minute! Can't we just give them an XBOX 360?! *(beat)* An XBOX CCCLX.

*(**HECTOR** looks to **ANTENOR**, who shrugs. **PARIS** becomes **AGAMEMNON**.)*

F1-ANTENOR. Worth a shot. I'll take the offer to Agamemnon.

*(All watch as **ANTENOR** crosses to **AGAMEMNON**, who considers the offer then slits **ANTENOR**'s throat. **AGAMEMNON** and **ANTENOR** exit.)*

M2-HECTOR. I'll take that as a "no."

*(**HECTOR** becomes **HERA**. **M1** enters.)*

M1-NARRATOR. <u>BOOK EIGHT!</u> Achilles sits in his tent. Meanwhile, up in Olympus, Hera was dismayed at the turn of events.

M2-HERA. That's it. I'm helping the Greeks. I don't care what Zeus says.

*(**IRIS** [F2] appears with telegram.)*

F2-IRIS. Iris here, Messenger of the Gods. I have a message for Hera!

M2-HERA. Give it here.

F2-IRIS. Do you have some form of I.D.?

M2-HERA. I'll turn you into a toad.

F2-IRIS. Good enough.

*(**IRIS** hands her telegram and exits.)*

M2-HERA. *(reading)* "Don't even think about it. Love Zeus." Poop.

*(**HERA** becomes **ODYSSEUS**. **NARRATOR** [F1], **NESTOR** [M1] and **AGAMEMNON** [M3] enter.)*

F1-NARRATOR. BOOK NINE! The Greek army was in disarray and even wise old Nestor was losing faith.

M1-NESTOR. I think we should swallow our pride *(glares at **AGAMEMNON**)* and send Odysseus to Achilles and get him back in the battle.

*(**AGAMEMNON** exits and **NESTOR** becomes **ACHILLES**.)*

F1-NARRATOR. Odysseus presented the case for returning to battle in the classic oratorical form, first with the opening statement, known as the Exordium.

M2-ODYSSEUS. Achilles, you are truly the greatest and mightiest of warriors. It is a privilege to be in your tent, to gaze upon your noble countenance, to smell your… earthy aroma.

F1-NARRATOR. Next, Odysseus presented the Narratio.

M2-ODYSSEUS. As you may know, our army is in peril of defeat. We need our best warrior.

F1-NARRATOR. Then Odysseus wrapped up his presentation with the Conformatio, also known as the Domo Arrigato Mister Roboto.

M2-ODYSSEUS. Agamemnon is offering you a real sweet

deal, so whattaya' say?

F1-NARRATOR. Achilles responded with the classic oratorical reply known as the Maximo Refuto.

*(**ACHILLES** gives the raspberry. **NARRATOR** [F2], **SLEEPING TROJAN #2** [F1] and **DIOMEDES** [M3] enter. **ACHILLES** becomes **SLEEPING TROJAN #1**.)*

F2-NARRATOR. BOOK TEN! With Achilles refusal, Odysseus and Diomedes were sent to spy on the sleeping Trojans.

M3-DIOMEDES. Diomedes rules!

M2-ODYSSEUS. Great. They'll hear us coming a mile away.

M3-DIOMEDES. *(whispering)* Diomedes rules…

*(Wakes a **TROJAN**.)*

M2-ODYSEEUS. Shhh. We won't harm you. We just need information.

M1-SLEEPING TROJAN #1. Well…I don't know what to tell you besides there's about 400 of us arranged in a horseshoe formation with some archers scattered around, but a lot of them are out of arrows so they're not much use. Oh, and there's some new troops from Thrace out on our flank who are sleeping unprotected.

F2-NARRATOR. Diomedes and Odysseus then killed the soldier.

(They do.)

M3-DIOMEDES. Diomedes ru…HEY! Wait. That doesn't seem very noble.

M2-ODYSSEUS. Yeah. We're noble and good. What's our motivation exactly?

F2-NARRATOR. That's what it says in the book. *(They continue:)* They then proceeded to the Trojan flank and killed all the sleeping warriors.

M2-ODYSSEUS. Wait a minute! This is completely out of character! The writer totally lost the tone here.

M3-DIOMEDES. Uncool.

F2-NARRATOR. You know, there are a lot of out-of-work

Greek heroes who would love this gig! Understand?

(They look at each other then continue killing. **SLEEPING DEAD TROJANS** *exit.)*

Then Odysseus and Diomedes returned to the Greek camp, where they cleansed the foul deeds of the night…together…in a ritual bath.

M3-DIOMEDES. Aw Come on!

M2-ODYSSEUS. This is shameless! I'm not a piece of meat! That's it! I don't care what the book says. Moving on!

M3-DIOMEDES. Moving on!

*(***ODYSSEUS** *exits.)*

F2-NARRATOR. Fine! **BOOK ELEVEN!** With valuable strategic information, Diomedes and the Greeks pushed the Trojans back.

M3-DIOMEDES. For the Glory of Greece! Diomedes Rules!

F2-NARRATOR. But the tide turned against the Greeks again. Even Paris scored a victory, wounding Diomedes.

*(***PARIS** *[M3] shoots an arrow into* **DIOMEDES** *[M3] foot.)*

M3-DIOMEDES. Diomedes is hit! Diomedes is down.

M3-PARIS. Paris rules!

*(***PARIS** *exits.* **PATROKLOS** *[F1] and* **ACHILLES** *[M1] enter.)*

F2-NARRATOR. Meanwhile Patroklos was trying to reason with Achilles.

F1-PATROKLOS. Achilles, I know you're yearning to rejoin the fray. Why don't you go back?

M1-ACHILLES. I don't care about that anymore. I'm busy redecorating my tent. Maybe I'll put some trimming on the cooking pot.

F1-PATROKLOS. Actually, that's the waste pot.

M1-ACHILLES. *(beat)* Maybe I'll order pizza tonight.

*(***PATROKLOS** *becomes* **NARRATOR,** *then* **TROJAN COMMANDER. F2** *and* **M3** *enter as soldiers. Eagle on a string*

crosses carried by **M1**, *who exits.)*

F1-NARRATOR. **BOOK TWELVE!** The Trojans continued to push the Greeks back when a Trojan Commander spotted something in the sky.

F1-TROJAN COMMANDER. Look! An eagle with a snake in it's talons! It's an omen of defeat for us!

M3-TROJAN SOLDIER #1. No, no! It's an omen of defeat for the Greeks!

F2-TROJAN SOLDIER #2. No, it's a sign the Gods are displeased with our sacrifices.

F1-TROJAN COMMANDER. No, you're thinking of an eagle with a *fish* in its talons. *That* means the Gods are displeased.

M3-TROJAN SOLDIER #1. No, that's the condor with the muskrat. Unless the muskrat is black, then it means four more weeks of winter.

(**POSEIDON** *[***M1***] enters with black tape on his finger holding it up as a moustache.* **TROJAN SOLDIER #1** *[***M3***] becomes* **GREEK SOLDIER #1**. **TROJAN SOLDIER #2** *becomes* **NARRATOR**.*)*

F2-NARRATOR. Despite their confusion, in **BOOK THIRTEEN** the Trojans again pushed the Greeks back to the sea. However, Poseidon, wearing a disguise, went among the Greeks offering encouragement.

M1-POSEIDON. Attaboy! Keep up the good work! You're doing great!

M3-GREEK SOLDIER #1. Ah, stranger. You are kind, but how I wish the Gods would help us.

M1-POSEIDON. *(showing disguise)* It's me! Poseidon!

M3-GREEK SOLDIER #1. Poseidon himself! Mighty Sea God, will you crush the Trojans with a tidal wave? Or command a terrible sea serpent to smite them?

M1-POSEIDON. Actually, I was just sort of walking through the ranks, offering encouragement, that sort of stuff.

M3-GREEK SOLDIER #1. That's it? You're the God of the Sea and that's it?! Jeez...you're about as useful as Aquaman! That's it boys, we're outa' here!

(POSEIDON *and* **TROJAN COMMANDER** *exit as* **ODYSSEUS** *[***M2***] enters.)*

M2-ODYSSEUS. Quit the battle? We cannot! It would be dishonorable and an insult to our fallen comrades! We must stay! Our country, our pride, our heritage demands it! *(sheepishly)* ...and...I lost the keys to the boat.

M3-GREEK SOLDIER #1. What?! Oh man!

M2-ODYSSEUS. Hey, it's not like these things have pockets! They must have fallen out into the sand somewhere.

M3-GREEK SOLDIER #1. Well, where's the last place you had them?

M2-ODYSSEUS. If I knew that, they wouldn't be lost, would they?

F2-NARRATOR. **BOOK FOURTEEN** is just a lot of arguing, so let's go to **BOOK FIFTEEN!** Patroklos confers with Nestor.

(PATROKLOS *[***F1***] and* **NESTOR** *[***M1***] enter.)*

F1-PATROKLOS. Nestor. How's the battle going?

M1-NESTOR. This is no *battle.* In my day, there were real fighters, not like these sissies today. We didn't have fancy armor or swords. No! We were naked! And we had rocks!

F1-PATROKLOS. Right. Anyway...

M1-NESTOR. Not even rocks! Pebbles! And you didn't stand far away and throw them either! No sir! You stood toe to toe with your enemy and you PUSHED the pebbles right into their flesh!

F1-PATROKLOS. Alright I get it! But how is it going NOW?

M1-NESTOR. Now? Not so good. We could really use that crybaby Achilles. If the men could just see him, it would really pick them up. Say! You're about his size. If you put on his armor and ride into battle, I bet that'd be just as good!

F1-PATROKLOS. That's not a bad idea. I'll go run it by Achilles.

(**NESTOR** *becomes* **ACHILLES.**)

F2-NARRATOR. BOOK SIXTEEN! Patroklos pleads with Achilles.

F1-PATROKLOS. Achilles! We need you! If you don't come back, at least let *me* wear your armor. The men will think it's you and be unstoppable!

M1-ACHILLES. Oh foolish youth, there's much more to being a great warrior than bravery and a fine suit of armor. You need...*(thinks)*...well there's also...*(stumped)*... Yeah, I guess all you need is bravery and armor. Go for it.

(**PATROKLOS** *dons Achilles armor.* **HECTOR** *[M2] enters followed by* **TROJAN SOLDIER #1** *[M3].* **NARRATOR** *will cross, remove* **PATROKLOS'** *helmet and exit.)*

F2-NARRATOR. Indeed, Patroklos bravely led the Greeks and was so courageous, his men truly believed he was Achilles, and so did the Trojans. But then his helmet fell off.

M2-HECTOR. Hey, you're not Achilles! You're that Patricide guy! Taste my steel, Greek dog! *(he kills* **PATROKLOS** *who dies onstage)* Ha! Got ya! Come on boys! Let's string up the body and mutilate it as a warning to the Greeks.

M3-TROJAN SOLDIER #1. A warning about what?

M2-HECTOR. A warning that if they kill us, we'll kill them!

M3-TROJAN SOLDIER #1. Isn't that what we've been doing for close to ten years now? I don't think mutilating one more body is going to make them quit.

M2-HECTOR. *(frustrated)* It's *tradition* and we're going to do it!

F1-NARRATOR. BOOK SEVENTEEN!

(**MENELAOS** *[M1] enters.)*

M1-MENELAOS. Not so fast. I, Menelaos, am here to retrieve Patroklos' body for a proper Greek burial.

M2-HECTOR. You will not take this body, Greek swine!

(**MENELAOS** *pulls a gun!!!! scaring the Trojans offstage.* **MENELAOS** *becomes* **ACHILLES**.)

F1-NARRATOR. The Greeks prevailed and took back poor Patroklos. **BOOK EIGHTEEN!** Achilles is told of Patroklos' death.

M1-ACHILLES. Nooooo! Why???? He was like a brother to me! My blood was his blood! My flesh was his flesh! We were as one! *(softly, reverently)* Why, I remember when we were just young lads frolicking in the fields and we'd…

F1-NARRATOR. *(cutting him off)* And so Thetis, seeing her son…

M1-ACHILLES. Whoa whoa whoa! I'm not done. I worked on this a long time. I drew on my emotional reserves. I used my sense memory!

F1-NARRATOR. Great. Time limit! So! Thetis sees her son's distress…

(**THETIS** *[***F2***] enters.)*

F2-THETIS. Oh my child. Why do you grieve so?

M1-ACHILLES. She won't let me do my big monologue.

F2-THETIS. *(slapping back of his head)* ACHILLES, why do you MOURN?

M1-ACHILLES. Patroklos is dead. I shall avenge him! *(trying again)* He was like a brother to me! I remember when we were young lads frolicking in the fields…

F2-THETIS. My son, you know that if you return to battle the Trojans, you are fated to die yourself.

M1-ACHILLES. I don't care. I will avenge Patroklos! *(trying yet again)* He was like a brother to me…

F2-THETIS. That's nice. I'll be right back.

(**THETIS** *crosses to entering* **HEPHAESTUS** *[***M3***].)*

Clever Hephaestus, I need you to fashion a suit of

armor for Achilles, the finest you can make.

M3-HEPHAESTUS. Goddess, I'm up to my tuchus in orders. Every big-wig on Olympus wants a super-duper helmet or shield or codpiece for their favorite soldier.

F2-THETIS. Please…

M3-HEPHAESTUS. *(old softy gives in)* Come by tomorrow after three. I'll see what I can do.

*(**HEPHAESTUS** and **THETIS** exit, leaving **ACHILLES** and **PATROKLOS**.)*

M1-ACHILLES. *(trying still yet again)* Ah noble comrade, you were like a brother to me. I remember when we were young lads frolicking in the fields… …

*(**PATROKLOS** reaches up and grabs **ACHILLES**. **GREEK SOLDIER #1** [M3] enters.)*

F1-PATROKLOS. Dude. Let it go.

M1-ACHILLES. *(to soldier)* Fine. Strip his clothes off. Wash his body. Put it in my tent.

M3-GREEK SOLDIER #1. Uh…okay.

M1-ACHILLES. *(shouting skyward)* I will avenge Patroklos! I will kill the miserable wretch Hector…NO MATTER WHAT!!!!

*(Dead **PATROKLOS** exits. **GREEK SOLDIER #1** becomes **NARRATOR**, then **AGAMEMNON**.)*

M3-NARRATOR. <u>BOOK NINETEEN</u> opens with the Greek camp preparing for the return of the mighty Achilles.

M3-AGAMEMNON. Men, I have some good news. Let's have a big fat Greek welcome back for…Achilles!

(SFX-wild applause)

M1-ACHILLES. Thank you, Agamemnon. I'd like to make a brief statement. *(beat)* Let's go kick some Trojan BUTT!!!!!!

(SFX-wild applause)

M3-AGAMEMNON. Thank you, Achilles. We're all glad you're back, but the men really need a rest and some food before we mount any sort of an attack. They've been going pretty hard. *(chuckle)* After all, not all of us have spent the past few months sitting around a tent getting fat.

M1-ACHILLES. What the hell is that supposed to mean?

M3-AGAMEMNON. Easy. Let's not get started again. Listen, just relax a bit. Maybe take a beach stroll with a pretty captured Trojan girl.

M1-ACHILLES. I am not eating or sleeping or strolling any beach until we have defeated the Trojans! While the troops rest I will commune with my noble steed.

*(**AGAMEMNON** exits as **ACHILLES** crosses to his entering **NOBLE STEED** [F1].)*

Oh faithful companion. How is it that you allowed valiant Patroklos to die while at your side?

F1-NOBLE STEED. Easy champ! First of all, he wasn't by my side. He was on top of me, okay? Second of all, what was I supposed to do? Fight hand to hand? Do you see any opposable thumbs here?

M1-ACHILLES. You should have carried him away. *(trying still yet again)* Patroklos was like a brother to me. I remember when we were just lads frolicking…

F1-NOBLE STEED. *(as actor)* I will kill you myself!

*(**NARRATOR** [M3] enters then becomes **HEPHAESTUS**. **APHRODITE** [F2] and **ARES** [M2] enter. **ACHILLES** becomes **ZEUS**. **NOBLE STEED** becomes **ATHENA**.)*

M3-NARRATOR. BOOK TWENTY! Back on Mount Olympus, Zeus called a council of the Gods.

M1-ZEUS. Alright people, it's come to my attention that a number of you have covertly been helping the Greeks or the Trojans.

(All start to protest.)

STOP. I'm omnipotent, for crying out loud. I know how everything turns out before it happens, which takes a lot of the fun out of the Olympics.

Anyway, I'm tired of fighting you all about it, and we need to make sure Achilles doesn't overstep his bounds. So, you can help whoever you want. Just be home by curfew. Go!

*(**ZEUS** becomes **ACHILLES**. **ARES** becomes **NARRATOR**.)*

M2-NARRATOR. BOOK TWENTY ONE! Hello everyone and welcome to the Greeks versus the Trojans, or as we like to call it, "The Brawl by the Wall."

We've got a great battle tonight. Assisting the Greeks will be some of Mount Olympus' finest such as Hera, Athena */**F1**/*, Poseidon, Hermes and Hephaestus */**M3**/*.

But the Trojan's immortal line-up is also quite impressive and alliterative, with Ares /**M2**], Apollo, Artemis and Aphrodite */**F2**/*.

And here comes Achilles */**M1**/* right out of the gate and it looks like he's moving in for a kill, but WAIT! Ares */**M2**/* swoops in with a spectacular save! Let's see that again in Slo-Mo instant replay! *(replay with **NARRATOR** as **ARES** blocking sword with beer can)*

But Achilles isn't letting this setback affect him as he just sweeps through the Trojan lines, slaughtering everyone in his path.

Now he's got the Trojans backed up to the River Xanthos... Hold on. The River God */**F1**/* is rising up and, yes, I believe it's, YES! he's doing a River Dance. The waves are rising and driving Achilles back!

But here comes Hephaestus */**M3**/*... and he's BOILING the river away with fire. Just look at that teamwork!

Now, Achilles has cornered Agenor */**F2**/*, half-brother of Hector.

WAIT A MINUTE! AGENOR is stepping forward. Agenor is actually going to have a soliloquy. Very unusual strategy for a minor character!

F2-AGENOR. I'm just here to foreshadow the battle between Achilles and Hector in the next chapter.

M2-NARRATOR. WOW! A bit player up from the minors and he hits it out of the park! But it looks like Achilles is going to kill him anyway.

F2-AGENOR. Ohhh!

M2-NARRATOR. Now it looks like the Trojans are retreating inside the city walls. They're all inside…

No, wait, there's one lone man standing outside the wall.

IT'S HECTOR *[***M2***]*! IT'S HECTOR!

So this is what it all comes down to folks.

One on one. Man to man. Achilles versus Hector for all the marbles!

F2-NARRATOR. <u>**BOOK TWENTY TWO!**</u>

F2-TROJAN. Courageous Hector, Come inside the walls and be safe!

M2-HECTOR. Nay I say. My family, my friends. I must stand my ground and face Achilles. I am a Trojan and fear nothing.

*(***ACHILLES** *roars with rage.* **HECTOR** *shrieks. They begin to run marathon style and grab cups handed to them by* **M3** *as they pass.)*

F2-NARRATOR. And so Achilles pursued Hector, three times they ran around the city walls.

*(***HECTOR** *stops and faces* **ACHILLES***.)*

M2-HECTOR. Alright! We battle to the death. Just promise me you will treat my corpse with respect should you prevail.

M1-ACHILLES. I make no deals with low-born Trojans, Hector! Your body will be mutilated as you would have done to Patroklos. He was like a brother to me. *(a final attempt at his monologue)* I remember when we were just lads frolicking…

(Group groan. **HECTOR** *screams and starts the battle. Grecian Urn pose. A comedic Matrix-style battle… moments of slo-motion and angle changes, etc…Finally, Hector is defeated.)*

M2-HECTOR. I am undone! My life slips like sand through an hourglass. I can recall when I was just a lad…

M1-ACHILLES. Oh no you don't! *(stabs* **HECTOR** *again)* If I don't get a monologue, no one does!

F2-NARRATOR. As Achilles stripped Hector of his armor and dragged his body off, the wails of sorrow could be heard for miles.

*(**CAST** exits making whale song leaving **ACHILLES** sitting in his tent and **HECTOR** as **NARRATOR**.)*

M2-NARRATOR. **BOOK TWENTY THREE!** That night, Achilles dreamt of his friend Patroklos and there was a funeral. Many horses were burned...don't ask.

*(**NARRATOR** exits and **ORACLE** [F1] enters.)*

F1-ORACLE. **BOOK TWENTY FOUR: THE FINAL BOOK!** Zeus sends Hermes with Priam to reason with Achilles.

*(**HERMES** [M3] and **PRIAM** [F2] enter and cross to **ACHILLES**.)*

M3-HERMES. Good King Priam of Troy. I am here to escort you safely to Achilles.

(They cross. **ACHILLES** *is startled and draws sword.)*

M1-ACHILLES. How did you get in here undetected?

M3-HERMES. Priam is under my protection. I am the benefactor of all travelers, ambassadors and florists. Ding!

F2-PRIAM. Achilles. Please return my son's body for a proper burial. Please. Think of your own father. Think of all the happy times you had with him. *(**ACHILLES** starts to mist up)* I remember him frolicking in the fields. He would look up to me and say, "Father, someday I will rule this kingdom as you have." But now those eyes will look at me…No more.

M1-ACHILLES. *(bawls then stops)* Wait a minute! How come you get a monologue but I don't?

M3-HERMES. She can act.

M1-ACHILLES. Alright, you win. You can have his body back. And to show there's no hard feelings, I'll call a truce and throw you a feast.

M3/F2-HERMES/PRIAM. Hooray!

(**HERMES** *and* **PRIAM** *exit.)*

F1-ORACLE. So there was a feast and a truce and Achilles learned an important lesson about humility and forgiveness. Thus, ends the Iliad…

M1-ACHILLES. That's the end? I'm still alive? Ha! In your face, Oracle!!

F1-ORACLE. However, one day later you die, when Paris shoots you with an arrow, which Apollo guides into your heel, which is your one vulnerable spot because…

M1-ACHILLES. …because that's where my mother held me when she dipped me in the River Styx to make me invulnerable…

F1-ORACLE. …which of course was the origin of the phrase…

M1-ACHILLES. *(leading audience)* …ACHILLES HEEL.

F1-ORACLE. Mama's boy.

M1-ACHILLES. If I die, then I'm takin' a death scene! I remember when...

F1-ORACLE. No. That's the end of Act I..I see in your future…Intermission!

(**ORACLE** *stops clock and exits.* **ACHILLES** *is alone onstage for a second. He looks at audience then exits.)*

End of Act I

ACT II

The Love Stories, Pt. 2

*(***EXPLOITATIS** *[***M3***] enters, starts clock again and steps forward, then sits.)*

(SFX -Agape Connection intro music.)

M3-EXPLOITATIS. Hi again, everybody and welcome to another episode of Agape *(ah-gah-pay)* Connection! The show that's all about the Hellenistic Hook-up. I'm your host, Exploitatis. Let's start with a real fun couple we got together last week. Give it up for Orpheus and Eurydice!

*(***ORPHEUS** *[***M1***] and* **EURYDICE** *[***F1***] enter and sit down.)*

So kids, tell us about your date.

F1-EURYDICE. Okay, so he's a musician, which is totally hot, and he plays this awesome lyre! I mean, we were in this bar and these dudes were fighting and Orpheus started playing and they totally stopped and just chilled.

M1-ORPHEUS. Yeah. I was blown away by how real she was. We hit it off and all, and things were going great until she got bit by this uptight viper and got summoned to the underworld.

M3-EXPLOITATIS. Bummer.

F1-EURYDICE. But he totally came and played the lyre until Cerberus went to sleep – all three heads!

M1-ORPHEUS. Hades himself said I could take her back... only I couldn't look at her until we reached the upper world. And man, we were almost back and she said, "Look, I'm back!" so of course I looked back and...

F1-EURYDICE. Dude, I said, "*Don't* look back, I'm not all the way up yet!"

M1-ORPHEUS. No you said, "Look."

F1- EURYDICE. There! You see! He did it again. You looked! He's a looker!

*(**ORPHEUS** and **EURYDICE** exit lightly squabbling.)*

M3-EXPLOITATIS. Well, it doesn't look like those two will be having a second date.

(SFX – Sitcom crowd laugh cutoff)

Let's see if we don't have better luck with our next couple. Let's have a hand for Pyramus and Thisbe!

*(**PYRAMUS** [M2] and **THISBE** [F2] enter.)*

Now, I understand you two have been having a secret fling going on for quite some time.

M2-PYRAMUS. Yes, that's true. We worked together and it would have been awkward if it had gotten out. So, we had to whisper to each other through a crack in the wall. But I finally threw caution to the wind and told her I wasn't going to hide anymore!

F2-THISBE. Oh yeah, real courageous. He told me to meet him at *midnight* behind the white mulberry bush. And he doesn't show up! No phone call, no note, nothing!

M2-PYRAMUS. I told you! I was an hour behind. My sundial stopped. There must have been an eclipse or something.

F2-THISBE. So I'm standing around waiting and this *lion* shows up with his mouth all bloody from whatever he just ate and I didn't want to be next, so I just ran out of there so fast my cloak flew off.

M2-PYRAMUS. Yeah, okay, but then *I* get there and see a lion running around with her bloody cloak in it's mouth! I was sure she was dead so, what else was I supposed to do? I killed myself.

F2-THISBE. Here's an idea: you say, "Hey, did anyone actually *see* the lion kill Thisbe?" You know, before you stick a knife in yourself!

M2-PYRAMUS. Ha! You did the same thing when you saw me dead!

F2-THISBE. I *saw* your body! I *knew* you were dead before I decided to punch my own ticket!

*(**PYRAMUS** exits in disgust.)*

M3-EXPLOITATIS. And that's why the mulberries are colored red; from the blood of the anguished lovers. Nice. So you two gonna have a second date?

F2-THISBE. We're dead, you idiot.

*(**THISBE** exits.)*

M3-EXPLOITATIS. Ouch. Okay, well thanks for playing.

(SFX – Sitcom crowd laugh cutoff)

Before we bring on our last couple, here's an update on one of our previous set-ups. It looked like Ceyx *(se'-iks)* and Alcyone *(al'-see-on)* weren't going to get that second date when they both died at sea, but the Gods intervened and turned them both into seagulls, so now they'll be flying and pooping together through eternity. Nice.

*(**PYGMALION** [**M1**] and statue of **GALATEA** [**F1**] enter.)*

Now this is an unusual set-up. Pygmalion, I understand you've made your *own* woman, correct?

M1-PYGMALION. Yessss. I've fashioned her from the finest marble. She is perfect in every way but one. She is not alive.

M3-EXPLOITATIS. Well have we got a surprise for you! Aphrodite!

*(**APHRODITE** enters and exits after waving a wand. **GALATEA** blinks to life and wraps her arms around **PYGMALION**.)*

F2-APHRODITE. Shazam!

M1-PYGMALION. She's alive!

M3-EXPLOITATIS. That's right, Pygmalion, a woman made exactly as you wish, who exists only to please and serve you, who will agree with your every thought and demand. This must be your dream come true!

M1-PYGMALION. She's perfect! Too perfect!!! I'm not good enough for her! *(pulling away)* She'll find another and leave me! I'll be alone then, a sad old man with only my memories of what might have been. It's too much, just too too much!

*(**PYGMALION** stabs himself with his chisel and dies. **GALATEA** shrugs and hangs on **EXPLOITATIS**.)*

M3-EXPLOITATIS. Guess there's not going to be a second date on that one either.

(SFX – Sitcom crowd laugh cutoff)

But that's okay, I'm sure we'll have better luck on the next episode of...Agape Connection!

Greek Hero Idol & Sports

(SFX-Agape Connection outro music fades into upbeat intro music. **ZEUS** *[M1],* **HERA** *[M2] and* **APHRODITE** *[F2] sit on Olympus.* **ANNOUNCER** *[F1] intros then exits.)*

F1-ANNOUNCER. Welcome to the final episode of…Greek Hero Idol!! Over the last 26 weeks our judges Zeus, Hera & Aphrodite have been auditioning the finest myths, legends and archetypes that Greece has to offer and we are now down to the final contestants!

*(***JASON** *[M3] enters.)*

M3-JASON. It is I, Jason of the Argonauts! Triumphant victor of many exciting voyages! I have captured the Golden Fleece and will now use it to reclaim the kingdom of my father from my cousin King Peleus.

M1-ZEUS. How'd you get the Fleece? And where are the other…what do you call them? Micronauts?

M3-JASON. Argonauts. Oh, they're off on their own adventures now. Anyway, we found this cool prophet, Phineas, and we chased away the harpies that kept stealing his food. So he warned us about the dangers we'd face on our voyage.

F2-APHRODITE. What kind of dangers?

M3-JASON. Well, for example, the clashing rocks *(demonstrates with his hands)*. But we went right through them without flinching!

M1-ZEUS. Right through?

M3-JASON. Well, we sent a dove through first to make sure it was safe…but it was a feisty dove, he was a handful! So then we passed an island full of fierce Amazons and the Rock of Prometheus.

M2-HERA. And did you battle these fierce Amazons?

F2-APHRODITE. Or aid poor Prometheus?

M3-JASON. Well, no…and no. See, we *woulda'* battled the Amazons, but it was late and Atalanta had a race and

Hercules was already gone looking for his friend. And we left Prometheus alone because, well, if Zeus says he's gotta get his liver eaten by a big eagle, hey, who are we to argue?

M1-ZEUS. Smart man.

M2-HERA. Suck-up.

M3-JASON. Anyhow, we made it to Colchis, where the Fleece was held by King Aeetes – don't ask me how to spell it. And then I saw his daughter, Medea and…

M1-ZEUS. *(To* **HERA***)* And that's when *you* butted in and made them fall in love.

M2-HERA. Well, me and Eros.

F2-APHRODITE. That's my boy!

M3-JASON. Man, I thought it was my aftershave. Anyway, the King was a butthead! He said I could have the Fleece if I yoked a couple of bronze, fire-breathing bulls, defeated an army that came from dragon's teeth and defeated the Terrible Snake that guarded the Fleece! So I did just that!

F2-APHRODITE. How exciting! And how did you do all that?

M3-JASON. Oh, it's real complicated, it involves a lot of strategy and math and tactical terms and…

M1-ZEUS. And Medea did a bunch of magic and pulled you through. Not good enough. There's always someone else doing the work for you. Isn't there Jason? I'm leaving. Call me when we get a real hero.

*(***ZEUS** *exits.)*

M3-JASON. Wait! Here's the cool part…I'm gonna' reclaim my throne. Hey Peleus, I've got the Fleece. The throne is mine!

*(***PELEUS** *[***M1***] enters.)*

M1-PELEUS. Too bad, I'm not giving it up.

M3-JASON. Oh yeah?!

*(***MEDEA** *[***F1***] enters with a plastic machete and cuts up* **PELEUS***, shoving him offstage.)*

M2-HERA. Jason! Zeus is right. You didn't even kill Peleus yourself. Medea did it. I'm sorry Jason, you're just not the next Greek Idol.

F2-APHRODITE. Nice job though.

M3-JASON. This blows!

(**MEDEA** *takes his arm and they start to exit.)*

F1-MEDEA. That's all right, honey, I can be your queen now.

M3-JASON. Uh, about that. I sorta married someone else.

F1-MEDEA. What?! Oh, I am *so* killing her with a robe of fire.

(They exit. **PERSEUS** *[***M1***] enters.)*

M1-PERSEUS. Hi, I'm Perseus. I'm one of Zeus' mortal off-spring. He came to my mom as an inspirational shaft of radiant light. But don't hold that against me okay?!

M2-HERA. Really?!

F2-APHRODITE. Okay, what do you have for us, Perseus?

M1-PERSEUS. Well, I need a really cool present for my step-dad's wedding, so I'm gonna cut off the head of Medusa, the Gorgon.

M2-HERA. Without turning to stone? This I have to see.

(**HERMES** *enters with shield and sword. Medusa's head [***F1** *holding and making monster noise] appears.)*

M3-HERMES. It is I, Hermes. The Gods wish to aid you in this quest. I bring a sword which cuts through all and Athena sends this shiny shield to see Medusa indirectly and here's a box to carry the head in.

M1-PERSEUS. All right, let's do this!

(**PERSEUS** *cuts her head off which falls in the box which he covers proudly with the shield.)*

M3-HERMES. Well, that's one way to get "Ahead!"

(**HERMES** *exits.)*

F2-APHRODITE. Nicely done, Perseus, *but…*

M2-HERA. You killed a Snake Lady with some divine tools. Sorry. *(to* **APHRODITE***)* It just doesn't have that "epic" touch. They never learn.

*(***PERSEUS** *exits sighing. Quick change to* **ZEUS** *[***M1***] who re-enters.)*

M1-ZEUS. Did I miss anything?

M2-HERA. Just another of your sons. An inspirational shaft of radiant light? You never come to *me* as an inspirational shaft of radiant light.

*(***HERA** *exits peeved.)*

M1-ZEUS. Next!

*(***THESEUS** *[***F1***] enters.)*

F1-THESEUS. I am Theseus, son of King Aegeus. I have sailed with Jason and the Argonauts. I have lifted the mighty rock my father hid the sword under, to prove my strength, and I have killed all the highway robbers on my way to Athens.

M1-ZEUS. And for that, Triple A thanks you. What do you have for us today?

F1-THESEUS. Today I'm going to go into the Labyrinth and slay the Minotaur to prevent fourteen Athenian citizens from being sacrificed to King Minos.

F2-APHRODITE. But no one has ever found their way out of the labyrinth.

F1-THESEUS. But I will! And that will make me…the Greatest Greek Hero!

(He approaches the labyrinth as **ARIADNE** *[***M2***] enters with a ball of string.)*

F1-THESEUS. Ariadne! Did Daedalus tell you how to get out of the maze?

M2-ARIADNE. He said unravel this string as you go in, then follow it back out.

F1-THESEUS. Brilliant! And now I, brave Theseus, go into the labyrinth!

(The **MINOTAUR** *[M3] enters and stands in the middle of the audience.* **THESEUS** *unwinds the string as he walks into the audience and confronts the* **MINOTAUR** *as* **ARIADNE** *exits. The* **MINOTAUR** *growls and says "moo.")*

F1-THESEUS. Now I shall defeat you with nothing but my fists!

M3-MINOTAUR. Just as well. For I am an unholy offspring of King Minos' wife and Poseidon's prize bull. My life is one of misery *(emotive cry of grief)* oh my God.

F1-THESEUS. No eliciting sympathy from the audience!

*(***THESEUS** *strikes and kills the* **MINOTAUR** *who exits.* **THESEUS** *reverses course through the maze and presents himself to* **ZEUS**.*)*

I have defeated the evil Minotaur! Ta-da!

M1-ZEUS. Ta-da? You cheated! Ariadne helped you.

F1-THESEUS. No one has EVER escaped from the labyrinth!

F2-APHRODITE. True. But Daedulus and his son Icarus are going to escape later *without* string. Daedulus is going to build wings from nothing and they fly out.

F1-THESEUS. But Icarus is going to fly too high, blind himself and when the wax melts he'll fall and die!

M1-ZEUS. So what?! They're not here competing to be the Greek Idol. I'm sorry. It's a no.

F1-THESEUS. I don't need this stupid contest anyway. I'm gonna go establish a commonwealth government.

M1-ZEUS. Yeah, well, good luck with *that.*

(SFX-sports show music. **ZEUS** *becomes* **ANNOUNCER** *[M1]. As he talks,* **ARACHNE** *[F1],* **AESCULAPIUS** *[F2],* **SISYPHUS** *[M2] and* **MIDAS** *[M3] enter and play cards.)*

M1-ANNOUNCER. We interrupt your current program with this sports update.

Outside Caesar's palace in the Temple of Jimmy the Greek, we've got a great poker tournament taking place.

At the final table so far, the Giants Otus and Ephialtes have bluffed each other right out of the game, Castor and Pollux busted out and are watching from the skybox and Bellerophon actually quit the game to go bet the ponies on a longshot, Pegasus at 12-1.

We're down to just four players, here we go...

(Players act out his actions as he says them.)

Arachne takes two cards and is weaving together a nice little hand...

Aesculapius opens the betting. His chip stack took quite a beating early on, but he's healed it nicely, (being the son of Apollo will do that for you)

Sisyphus has had an uphill battle at this table. He pushes his chips into the pot...and now they're rolling back and he's pushing them back in, and now they're rolling back, this could go on for a while...but wait...it looks like King Midas has just raised everyone right out of the game! Wow, where'd he get all those gold chips? Very exciting!

And now we take you back to Greek Hero Idol!

(SFX- music. **ANNOUNCER** *becomes* **ZEUS**. **SISYPHUS** *becomes* **HERA**. *Other players exit.* **PHAETHON** *[***F2***] enters.)*

M1-ZEUS. All right, let's pick us a hero! Who do we got?

F2-PHAETHON. I am Phaethon and the Sun is my father. He swore by the river Styx to grant any wish I have. So I'm going to drive the Chariot of the Sun!

M2-HERA. Mortal, this is folly! No one can drive that except the Sun!

F2-PHAETHON. But I shall! And I shall bring night and day to Mother Earth! Horses!

(**F1** *and* **M3** *bring on hobby horses and ride around until* **PHAETHON** *loses control then they exit in the blackout.)*

The Heavens are amazing! Look there's Leo! And Cancer! Oh, he looks mad! Faster, horses! Faster! Oh, it's too fast! I can't hold it together! I'm crashing! I'm breaking up! I'm breaking up! AAAH!

(Blackout. SFX – Explosion. **PHAETHON** *leaves beanie behind in front of judges and becomes* **APHRODITE***.)*

M2-HERA. Sadly, thus is the fate of all mortals who attempt the Deeds of Gods.

M1-ZEUS. You speak truly. *(a beat)* He signed the waiver, right?

M2-HERA. Yep.

M1-ZEUS. Good, we're covered. Next!

(**M3-HERCULES** *enters.)*

M3-HERCULES. Hi, my name is Hercules. *(crushes Styrofoam cup)*

JUDGES. Hello Hercules.

M3-HERCULES. Before you judge me, let me just say I know I've got some anger management issues.
I threatened to beat up the sea and shoot the sun.
And I know when I get in one of my moods, I accidentally kill some people...like my wife and kids.
But I don't think that's unusual considering when I was a baby somebody put *snakes* in my crib 'cause they were mad at my mom for fooling around with Zeus.

(**ZEUS** *glares at* **HERA***.)*

M2-HERA. I was out of town at the time.

M3-HERCULES. I know that's no excuse for my anger. So I went to my cousin King Eurystheus to find out how I could cleanse myself. He gave me kind of a twelve-step program. He called them the Labors of Hercules.
First, I choked the lion of Nimea,
then slew the nine-headed serpent Hydra,
then I captured Artemis's Golden Stag, alive mind you.
I also nabbed a great mountain boar.
Then, in one day I cleaned the Aegean Stables.

M1-ZEUS. There's over a thousand cattle in there. Phew!

M3-HERCULES. Tell me about it, I had to bend *two* rivers to clean it out.

Lets see what else. Oh I remember!
I drove away the Stymphalian birds,
captured the Cretan Bull,
disposed of the man-eating horses of Diomedes…

M2-HERA/F2-APHRODITE. Diomedes Rules!

M3-HERCULES. Charmed Hippolyta's girdle away from her – and incidentally, she ain't called HIPpolyta for nothing -
brought back the Cattle of Geryon,
retrieved the Apples of Hesperides,
took Atlas' place for a day,
freed Prometheus as a bonus,
and finally brought Cerberus the three-headed dog up from Hades.
I AM AWESOME!

M1-ZEUS. Wow, now *that* is a Great Greek Hero! *(To* **M2-HERA***)* Hon, what do you think?

M2-HERA. *(aghast)* He *killed* his *wife* and *children.*

M1-ZEUS. *(beat, resolved)* Sorry, Big Guy, it's gonna be a "No."

M3-HERCULES. Man, make *one* little mistake…

*(***HERCULES** *exits. SFX – sports music. Announcer [***F2***] enters. As she talks, actors bring in the grease board and arrange themselves around it.* **TANTALUS** *[***F1***] has a ball cap and whistle.)*

F2-ANNOUNCER. Let's take another quick break from Greek Idol and hop over to ESPN V. I., that's ESPN 6 – and check on the big Tragedy Face-off.
First, let's go to the locker room of the House of Atreus and Coach Tantalus.

F1-TANTALUS. *(diagramming, pointing to people as he speaks)* All right, let's focus!
To start the game, I'm gonna boil my son Pelops and serve him to the Gods to prove they can be fooled.
They're gonna send me to Hades.
Niobe, you step in and turn into a weeping stone because of your pride. This will catch 'em off guard.

We know our bread and butter is when Iphigenia is sacrificed to get the ships underway in the Iliad.

Next, Orestes, you're her brother; you execute a surprise attack on her Mom;

and Electra, just keep mourning, it becomes you.

We're the underdogs here, there are a lot of people who think we're gonna give 'em a happy ending… let's go prove 'em wrong!

(Actors huddle and shout, "TRAGEDY!" Actors shift position.)

F2-ANNOUNCER. Now let's go to the locker room of the House of Thebes and Coach Oedipus.

(Same action as before.)

M3-OEDIPUS. Alright you flesh-eating dirt popsicle maggots!

First King Laius is going to marry his cousin and have me.

Then he'll leave me in the wilderness to die because it's foretold that I'll kill him.

In a trick-play double-reverse, I won't recognize Laius and accidentally kill him, I'll solve the Sphinx's riddle making me a hero and go marry my own mother, Jocasta.

Apollo, you're gonna send a plague on us until Tiresias tells me I killed Dad and married Mom.

Jocasta commits suicide.

I blind myself and wander for years.

Now, this is a very unconventional strategy so I need everyone to know their assignments! Now let's go out there and KILL THEM!!! Let us pray.

(Exit leaving **ZEUS, ODYSSEUS** *and* **ANNOUNCER** *onstage.)*

F2-ANNOUNCER. There you have it sports fans, the inside scoop.

The House of Athens was disqualified after testing

positive for artificial Dramatic Irony, leaving us with this great showdown between Thebes and Atreus.

Now we want to jump back to Greek Idol, where I believe they've just crowned the winner…and it's… Odysseus!

*(**SFX** -cheering.)*

*(**ZEUS** shakes **ODYSSEUS**' hand. **ANNOUNCER** crosses to them. **ZEUS** exits.)*

M1-ZEUS. Congratulations! Bravery! Cunning! Adventure! Smarts! Character Arc! AND Romance! Plus only a little godly assistance! You really deserve it! I made the right choice. I'm really smart.

F2-ANNOUNCER. Odysseus, you are the Greek Idol! The Greatest Greek Hero of all. How do you feel right now?!!!

M2-ODYSSEUS. Wow, I don't …

F2-ANNOUNCER. That's great! For our viewers just tuning in on the West Coast, why don't you recap your story?

M2-ODYSSEUS. My story! Wow… where do I start?

F2-ANNOUNCER. Well, we know about your exploits in the Iliad, why don't you pick up with the end of the Trojan War.

M2-ODYSSEUS. Okay!

*(**SOLDIER** [F1] enters as **ANNOUNCER** exits)*

The Trojan Horse

F1-SOLDIER. Explain it to me again.

M2-ODYSSEUS. Okay. We're building this big horse and we're going to leave it here and all the ships are going to sail out of sight, except most of us are actually going to hide inside the horse.

F1-SOLDIER. I get that part.

M2-ODYSSEUS. When the Trojans see us retreating, they run down here to see what's going on and destroy everything left behind.

F1-SOLDIER. I get that too. But where am I again????

M2-ODYSSEUS. We leave you behind.

F1-SOLDIER. See that's what I thought you said. SO you're telling me the Trojans are going destroy everything left behind, and what's left behind is ME...

M2-ODYSSEUS. ...and the Horse.

F1-SOLDIER. AND MEEEEEE!!!!

M2-ODYSSEUS. Just tell them the story I told you!

F1-SOLDIER. Oh yeah...that'll work!

M2-ODYSSEUS. Dude. It's reverse psychology...trust me. Besides, it's a done deal. We're already inside and the ships are sailing and here come the Trojans. Be Cool!

*(***ODYSSEUS** *"climbs into" the diagrammed top of the Trojan Horse, under the grease board legs.* **TROJANS** *enter!)*

M3-TROJAN GUARD. Hey! Where did everyone go!?!

M1-TROJAN OFFICER. What's with the Big Hollow Wooden Horse and why are you here alone???

F1-SOLDIER. It's for Athena! The Greeks quit and hoped you would destroy it and bring a curse on yourself. I didn't want any part of it, so I escaped before they set sail.

(A sneeze from inside the horse.)

M1-TROJAN OFFICER. What was that sneeze?

F1-SOLDIER. Achoo!

M1-TROJAN OFFICER. And what's this extremely obvious hatch in the belly?

F1-SOLDIER. That's where the Greeks put the really big, hard to move, sacred… uhm… stuff … they wanted you to destroy.

M1-TROJAN OFFICER. I see.

M3-TROJAN GUARD. What do we do with him?

M1-TROJAN OFFICER. Oh right.

(He cuts **F1***'s throat, who exits.)*

F1-SOLDIER. Aww… c'mon! I knew it!

M1-TROJAN OFFICER. Roll this suspicious Giant Hollow Wooden Horse with the sneeze from inside and the belly hatch into the city. We will have a celebration to Athena in the morning, then turn it into a playground for the kids. Guard it tonight.

*(***TROJAN OFFICER** *leaves* **TROJAN GUARD** *standing guard. Dozens of men climb out of the horse one at a time and sneak past* **GUARD***. They can get louder and make mistakes [sneeze, loudly bump the horse, step on a rubber chicken, Thor exits, etc…] but* **GUARD** *never sees them or acknowledges anything is wrong. Finally,* **ODYSSEUS** *climbs out last and taps him on the shoulder, then kills* **GUARD***, who exits.)*

M3-TROJAN. Oh no! Reverse Psychology!

*(***ANNOUNCER** *[***F2***] returns.)*

M2-ODYSSEUS. And so we pillaged the city and killed everyone. Cassandra tried to warn them, but no one listens to her. Anyway, that's how the Greek Army won the war. Menelaos got Helen back and it took me another 10 years to finally get home.

F2-ANNOUNCER. And that's the Odyssey right?

M2-ODYSSEUS. That's right. Those 10 years getting home are the Odyssey. Homer preferred to write in flashback, but it's much easier for me to tell it chronologically.

F2-ANNOUNCER. Please do. *(points to clock)* And faster.

The Odyssey

(The men gather around.)

M2-ODYSSEUS. You stupid idiots. We wouldn't be lost at sea if you guys hadn't defiled Athena's temple.

F1-MAN. We thought you wanted to have Athena mad at us.

M2-ODYSSEUS. At the Trojans! And that was a lie to get us into the city, remember. And when we stopped to pillage the town of Cicones *(sick'-o-nees)*, what did I say?

F2-MAN. You said have fun!

M2-ODYSSEUS. I said, "Let's go before they reinforce and counterattack!" So then we have to make a hasty retreat to another island for repairs and we ended up in the land of the Lotus-eaters. What did I tell you about the Lotus?

F2-MAN. You said have fun!

M2-ODYSSEUS. I did NOT! Lotus makes you lose your mind, memory and desire to get ***home***. It's a gateway drug gang. You start taking Lotus, next thing you know you start craving ambrosia.

M3-MAN. Who's got ambrosia?!!!!

M2-ODYSSEUS. No one but the Gods! We lost dozens of men to Lotus. Don't you get it?! Any kind of drug is bad…

M3-MAN. Even…ambrosia?

F1-MAN. Isn't that fruit salad with jello and marshmallows?

ALL. I love that stuff. It's great! I wish we had some right now.

M2-ODYSSEUS. You guys NEVER LISTEN TO ME. I swear! You're all gonna end up dead at this rate. Pay attention! Okay?

(They all nod shamefully.)

The Cyclops

M2-ODYSSEUS. Okay. Here's what we're going to do now. We're a little short on supplies, so some of you are going to stay here on the boat and the rest of you are going to come with me.
There's an abnormally large cave on the mainland hillside over there. Clearly someone must live there.
We'll take them some wine and maybe they'll be kind enough to help us with some food for the trip.

(All exit and get as many men dolls as they can carry and enter and puppet them, except **M1** *who exits to become* **CYCLOPS**.*)*

M2-ODYSSEUS PUPPET. Wow. What a big cave. I wonder who lives here.

M1-CYCLOPS. I do! I am Polyphemus, son of Poseidon! Who are you?! What are you doing in my cave?!

M2-ODYSSEUES PUPPET. My name is…Nobody. We have traveled long and far and seek comfort and food under the traditional rules of Greek hospital…

*(***CYCLOPS** *picks up one of Odysseus's men and eats him. The men scream!)*

M1-CYCLOPS. You make a fine meal. Better than my sheep. You will be my guests for dinner. Ha ha ha ha ha!

PUPPET MEN. The door! Before he seals it! Run away!

*(***CYCLOPS** *seals the cave, picks another man up and eats him. The remaining dolls cower away.)*

M1-CYCLOPS. Goodnight Nobody.

*(***CYCLOPS** *falls asleep. Dolls circle up.)*

PUPPETS. Whisper whisper whisper. Whisper whisper. Aaaaaaand break!

M1-CYCLOPS. Daybreak! *(eats another doll)* And now to let my sheep roam free, but I will see you for dinner tonight!

*(***CYCLOPS** *leaves with dolls still trapped in cave.* **ODYSSEUS** *gives orders.)*

M2-ODYSSEUS PUPPET. Quick. We haven't much time. You men, sharpen that log to a point and put the tip in the fire.

(Puppeteering commences...lifting suction cup stick to platform. **CYCLOPS** *returns and eats another man.)*

M2-ODYSSEUES PUPPET. Oh Polyphemus, great Cyclops. Here wash down that man with a bit of wine we brought. It is strong.

M1-CYCLOPS. Not as strong as me! *(He rapidly drinks it all.)* Whoa...Good hooch!

*(***CYCLOPS*** passes out, falling asleep with head on table where puppets are. They quickly pick up the shaft and suction cup the arrow to his swim mask-eye.)*

M1-CYCLOPS. Argh!!!! Nobody tricked me! Nobody is killing me!!!!

*(***CYCLOPS*** tries to find the men as they run out past him and* **CYCLOPS** *exits. Full size men run back onstage.)*

M2-ODYSSEUS. Quick, row like your lives depended on it! Great Cyclops, you cannot see me, but hear my words! It wasn't Nobody who tricked you, it was I! Get it??? Eye? I?! *(laughing at his own joke)* Never mind...Tell your daddy it was me, Odysseus!

F1-MAN. That's a good one. Tell your daddy, POSIEDON, GOD OF THE SEA, it was me, the guy in the BOAT, who blinded you.

M2-ODYSSEUS. He's way back on land and blind. What can he do?

F2-MAN. Big boulder coming in boss.

(SFX -splash. Actors teeter.)

M2-ODYSSEUS. Row faster, to that island over there. I'll get us some food over there.

The Land of the Wind

*(**ODYSSEUS** crosses to meet **AEOLUS**.)*

M3-AEOLUS. I am Aeolus, Keeper of the Winds.

M2-ODYSSEUS. Great Aeolus. We have traveled far and faced many dangers. Your winds will carry us home.

M3-AEOLUS. Some will, but some aren't so good. Here is a sack with all my bad winds. *(SFX – he farts into a sack)* Now there will only be good winds left to guide you home.

M2-ODYSSEUS. Thank you. *(He returns to ship with the sack.)* The wind is ours now! Set sail for Ithaca! We'll be home soon!

M1-MAN. Hey, what's in the sack.

M2-ODYSSEUS. Nothing. Butt air.

MEN VARIOUS. Nothing but air. Right?! It's full. I bet it's treasure. I want my share.

M2-ODYSSEUS. Look! Land! At last we are home. I can finally rest. Wake me up when we dock. *(He nods off.)*

MEN VARIOUS. Now's our chance. Lets see the treasure! Open it quick!

*(SFX – Farts. Men are thrown around screaming and agonizing. **F1** exits in the commotion.)*

M1-MAN. It's not the smell so much as the burning of the eyes.

F1-MAN. Uh. Odysseus. Sorry, we opened your bag and your butt air threw us off course.

M2-ODYSSEUS. Let's row guys.

Circe the Enchantress

*(**CIRCE** [F1] enters.)*

F1-CIRCE. Yoo-hoo! Hello sailors!

M3-MAN. Odysseus, let us go ashore please!

M1-MAN. We've been rowing and rowing and rowing our boat…

F2-MAN. Gently across the sea…

M2-ODYSSEUS. Verily then, go on ashore!

F1-CIRCE. Life is but a dream!

*(**THE MEN** walk to her as she waves her wand, they squeal and turn to pigs as she leads them offstage.)*

M2-ODYSSEUS. Hmmm, they've been gone a while. I better go after them.

*(**HERMES** [M3] appears.)*

M3-HERMES. Are you going empty handed to Circe the Enchantress ?

M2-ODYSSEUS. Wily crafty Hermes! What do you suggest?

M3-HERMES. Flowers are always nice. Ding.

Oh, and eat a little of this antidote so she can't turn you into a pig.

When you don't change, she'll be caught off guard.

You can threaten her and get anything you want.

*(**ODYSSEUS** eats a leaf as **HERMES** exits and **CIRCE** [F1] re-enters.)*

M2-ODYSSEUS. Cool. Hail Circe!

F1-CIRCE. Yes. I've been waiting for you. *(Waves wand. Nothing happens.)*

M2-ODYSSEUS. Hah! Where are my men?

F1-CIRCE. They're pigs!

M2-ODYSSEUS. I know, but where are they?

F1-CIRCE. No really. I turned them into pigs. If you want them back, you'll have to make love to me everyday for the next year!

M2-ODYSSEUS. Well. A man's gotta do what a man's gotta do! *(aside to audience)* One year later. Now help us get home?

F1-CIRCE. I can only tell you how to find the blind prophet Tiresias. He can tell you what you need to do to get home.

M2-ODYSSEUS. Deal. Oh, the Land of the Dead.

The Land of the Dead

(Light and SFX. The Dead approach on all sides surrounding **ODYSSEUS**. *They are:* **TIRESIAS** *[***F1** *with dark sunglasses],* **AGAMEMNON** *[***M3** *w/arrow through the head],* **ACHILLES** *[***M1** *] and* **ODYSSEUS' MOTHER** *[***F2** *in a shawl over her head].)*

ALL. Odysseus. Hear our words.

M2-ODYSSEUS. Tell me souls. Help me get home. Tiresias, why is my journey so long?

F1-TIRESIAS. You pissed off Poseidon by blinding his son. Duh! A blind man could see that one coming! Be smarter from now on and you'll get home.

M2-ODYSSEUS. That's it. Be smarter?

F1-TIRESIAS. Picky! Okay, tell your men not to eat the cattle of the Sungod or they'll all die.

F2-MOTHER. Son!

M2-ODYSSEUS. Mom? You're dead?

F2-MOTHER. Yeah. It's not so bad. You could visit a little more often.

M2-ODYSSEUS. Do you have any idea what I'm going through trying to get home, Ma?

F2-MOTHER. I'm just saying.

M3-AGAMEMNON. Odysseus!

M2-ODYSSEUS. Agamemnon! What are you doing here? I thought you got home after the war?

M3-AGAMEMNON. Yeah, well, remember when I killed my daughter so we could set sail and go to war? My wife Clytemnestra was kind of upset and assassinated me when I got home.

M2-ODYSSEUS. Bummer.

M3-AGAMEMNON. Tell me about it.

M1-ACHILLES. Hey dude!

M2-ODYSSEUS. Oh, hey, Achilles. *(baiting* **ACHILLES***)* Man, you were doing so great up there. What happened?

M1-ACHILLES. Paris shot me…in my Achilles' heel.

(Everyone laughs.)

M2-ODYSSEUS. Yeah, I thought so.

F1-TIRESIAS. How'd you not see that one coming?!

M1-ACHILLES. Like you're so smart!

M3-AGAMEMNON. Hey! Wear a boot or something man!

M1-ACHILLES. Take me back with you. This dead stuff is boring.

M2-ODYSSEUS. I bet. I'd definitely rather be alive and miserable than dead.

ALL. Take us back! Take us back! You never write, you never call. Etc…

M2-ODYSSEUS. I can't! I just can't! *(They all disappear. He looks around a moment)* Okay. I've got to be smarter. Men! Gather round.

The Choices

M2-ODYSSEUS. Men, here's our plan.

First, we have to go past the Sirens. Don't worry. You'll fill your ears with beeswax and tie me to the mast. And you row, really fast.

Then we go by the Charybdis, the whirlpool that sucks everything near it underwater 3 times a day, so again, we have to row really fast.

Then we face the terrible Scylla with 6-heads that will each eat a man. Probably shouldn't have told you that…just row really fast.

That's the plan. Let's go.

(They tie **ODYSSEUS** *up, stuff their ears with wax and start rowing in unison. SFX – Annoying Music of choice.* **ODYSSEUS** *screams!* **SCYLLA** *takes 2 men [***M1** *and* **F2***] leaving* **F1** *and* **M3** *terrified rowing extremely fast and slowing and slowing and slowing until they stop, then mime a post-orgasmic cigarette. They exit and re-enter as they cannot hear Odysseus' pleas with wax still in their ears.)*

MEN. That stank! I'm hungry. Look there's an island with cattle, let's eat!

M2-ODYSSEUS. Guys! Guys? Guys! Hey! Leave that cattle alone! EMPTY YOUR EARS! GUYS!

MEN. That was good. Was that brisket? Kobe! So good!

*(Zeus [***M1***] enters.)*

M1-ZEUS. EAT HOT SMITE!

(SFX – Thunder, then lightning as **ZEUS** *[***M1***] throws his foam thunderbolts. Men all die and* **ODYSSEUS** *is freed from his bonds, he swims until he washes ashore. He is weary, defeated and sobbing.* **CALYPSO** *[***F2***] enters.)*

Calypso

F2-CALYPSO. Welcome to Ogygia *(O-gidg-ia)*. I am the sea nymph goddess Calypso. You have nothing more to fear. I am alone here.

M2-ODYSSEUS. Please help me get home.

F2-CALYPSO. This shall be your new home. Come, you need rest, so you can restore your strength.

*(**ZEUS** [**M1**], **ATHENA** [**F1**] and **HERMES** [**M3**] walk onstage watching them.)*

F1-ATHENA. Daddy, seriously. We've got to let him get home.

M1-ZEUS. I know baby, but if we make her let Odysseus go, she'll make Uncle Poseidon kill him. We've got to let her have some fun first.

F1-ATHENA. For how long? I promised his son I'd help.

M3-HERMES. He doesn't look in that big a hurry to me. Calypso is hot! He's fine…

F1-ATHENA. How long, Daddy?

M1-ZEUS. I don't know. How long have those two been at it now Hermes?

M3-HERMES. *(impressed)* Seven years.

F1-ATHENA. Daddy! He has a wife and a son!

M1-ZEUS. Alright, alright. Hermes, go tell Calypso she has to let him go home.

M3-HERMES. You got it, boss.

*(**ZEUS** and **ATHENA** exit. **HERMES** goes to **CALYPSO** draped on a bored **ODYSSEUS**.)*

F2-CALYPSO. I love you.

M2-ODYSSEUS. No you don't. All you ever want is sex. Why can't we just talk?

F2-CALYPSO. All you ever want to talk about is home, and your wife…phhhft. If you marry me, I'll make you immortal.

M3-HERMES. Calypso. Zeus says let him go.

F2-CALYPSO. Hey! I live alone on an island. Where else am I supposed to find a husband?

M3-HERMES. Hey. Zeus says. That's how I roll.

(She stomps her foot and pouts offstage.)

She's been hiding the supplies you need to set sail on the other side of the island. You should be cool now. Good luck.

Oh, and Poseidon is visiting the Ethiopes. If you leave quick you might get home before he gets back and the drama queen cries to daddy.

M2-ODYSSEUS. Hurray!

*(**ODYSSEUS** sails. **POSEIDON** [**M1**] appears.)*

M1-POSEIDON. Where do you think you're going??!!!!

*(**POSEIDON** almost kills **ODYSSEUS** with trident and SFX – windstorm. **ODYSSEUS** ends up ashore as the **KING** [**M3**] and **QUEEN** [**F2**] of Phaecia enter.)*

The Phaecians

F2- QUEEN. Look darling. A man has drifted onto our shore. Should we help?

M3-KING. The poor soul. I think we should. You there! What is your name?

M2-ODYSSEUS. My name is a curse. I dare not say it or bring the wrath of Poseidon on you as well.

F2-QUEEN. Well that's sweet. He's thoughtful.

M2-ODYSSEUS. I only want to go home… *(meaningfully)* to my wife Penelope on the island of Ithaca.

F2-QUEEN. Hey. I know a Penelope of Ithaca. She's been missing a husband for almost 20 years now. Darling, what was his name?

M3-KING. Jerry.

F2-QUEEN. No, not Jerry. But it's like Jerry. Harry. Barry.

M2-ODYSSEUS. Odysseus.

F2-QUEEN. No, that's not it. Oh…was it Laertes?

M3-KING. From Hamlet?

F2-QUEEN. Oh no, that's his father.

M3-KING. Hamlet's father?

F2-QUEEN. No, the missing husband's father. He's been grieving until his son comes home. What was his name?

M2-ODYSSEUS. Odysseus.

F2-QUEEN. Wait a second. It'll come to me.

M2-ODYSSEUS. My name is Odysseus.

M3-KING. Hamlet's father was a ghost. I don't even think he had a name other than King of Denmark, because Hamlet was called the Prince of Denmark.

F2-QUEEN. Who's Hamlet?

M3-KING. I don't know. It hasn't been written yet.

M2-ODYSSEUS. My NAME is ODYSSEUS!

I fought in the Trojan War.

I traveled to the Land of the Winds and the Land of

the Dead.

I fought the Cyclops and the Scylla and Circe and Calypso and Poseidon!

I AM ODYSSEUS!!!!

M3-KING. Whoever you are stranger, I am the King of this land and you have my word, if you wish to return to Ithaca, I shall send you to Ithaca. And you shall take many gifts and riches from us, as you have entertained us on our way to the spa. Travel well, stranger.

*(***KING** *and* **QUEEN** *exit.* **ATHENA** *[***F1***] enters.)*

The Final Journey Home

F1-ATHENA. Odysseus. It is I, Athena. I come bringing this cloud as cover and when you awake you will be in Ithaca, but do not go home. It is not safe for you yet.

M2-ODYSSEUS. Blessed Goddess. What has become of my home? My wife?

F1-ATHENA. Your home is overrun with rude suitors trying to marry your wife.

She stalled them by weaving and unraveling a shroud for your dying father.

She could have continued, but for your disloyal maids, who told the suitors of her trick.

M2-ODYSSEUS. And what of my son Telemachus?

F1-ATHENA. He has just returned from his own great journeys searching for you.

He is hidden from the dangerous suitors in the shed of the swineherd.

Hide your treasure and go there.

I shall disguise you for protection until you are ready to claim your throne again.

(She hands him a shawl which he places over his head and shoulders.)

M2-ODYSSEUS. That's it?

F1-ATHENA. Well at least hunch over. They'll think you're a beggar. Trust me.

*(**ATHENA** exits. **ODYSSEUS** crosses to the entering **TELEMACHUS** [**M3**].)*

The Father/Son Reunion

M3-TELEMACHUS. Hello beggar. Come in.

M2-ODYSSEUS. You must be Telemachus.

M3-TELEMACHUS. Yes, but how did you… ?

M2-ODYSSEUS. *(pulls off shawl)* It's me, Odysseus, your father!

(They embrace.)

M3-TELEMACHUS. Dad! Boy did I miss you! I had to run the 3-legged race with Uncle Stumpius at the father/son picic.

M2-ODYSSEUS. I missed you too son. Take me back to the house. I'll be disguised. While I figure out what to do next, you hide all the weapons.

(He pulls up the cloak as all the others swirl around carousing loudly as suitors.)

The Suitors and the Old Dog

M2-ODYSSEUS BEGGAR. Drachma for a beggar? I don't want to fight, just please be kind. Help an old man?

(They treat him badly.)

SUITORS. Ha! Old beggar! No drachmas for beggars!! Sit out of our way…over there.

*(***ODYSSEUS*** is thrown down beside ***OLD DOG*** [M1].)*

M1-OLD DOG. What's this? That smell?

So rancid like an old beggar, yet so fresh compared to the dung I lay dying in here.

And so familiar. So familiar. It's been 20 years since I have smelt this. *(He sniffs Odysseus' crotch.)*

Is this my master returned?

20 years I have waited. That's 140 in dog years. Long ago I dreamt of this day.

You trained me to fetch and play, to sit and stay.

And I have stayed, true to you and this home, knowing you would return.

I shed a tear of contentment and joy.

I would leap to my feet if I could, but now, with my last doggy breath, I give the affection due to you master.

*(***OLD DOG*** licks ***ODYSSEUS***' face and dies. ***PENELOPE*** [F1] enters.)*

F1-PENELOPE. Who has thrown this old beggar in the dung? Have none of you respect for those less fortunate than yourself?

M3-SUITOR. Why should we show respect when we have been shown none? We have waited patiently. Surely Odysseus is dead. Tomorrow you must choose a new husband. Then we shall be kind to those who serve us.

F1-PENELOPE. Poop on you!

*(***SUITORS*** and ***OLD DOG*** exit.)*

The Plan and the Prayers

F1-PENELOPE. Sad old beggar. I am sorry these men have treated you so badly.

M2-ODYSSEUS. They insist you choose a suitor.

F1-PENELOPE. I choose Odysseus. Dead or alive he is better than all these men. I wait as long as I must and pray my son grows strong enough to defend himself.

M2-ODYSSEUS. Yet they insist. Your life is in danger now as well.

F1-PENELOPE. I have a plan. I shall announce that I shall only marry the man who can string Odysseus' bow and shoot an arrow through the handles of 12 axes. Only Odysseus can do that, so I shall not have to choose.

M2-ODYSSEUS. Good plan.

F1-PENELOPE. Thank you. *(beat)* Good night.

*(***PENELOPE** *exits.)*

M2-ODYSSEUS. And so it shall be. I shall string the bow and have my revenge on these foul 108 suitors. There are so many though. I shall have Telemachus at my side… he's good for 2 or 3, but what of the rest?

Athena. Good Goddess. I pray your aid. Help my hand be true and swift.

Zeus, greatest of all. I have traveled and now I am home because of you. You who look kindly on those lost and wandering. Grant me peace. Give me a sign that I shall prevail.

(SFX – Thunderbolt…Eagle flies by…thumbs up from the wings…Angel Choir. **ODYSSEUS** *smiles.)*

The Slaughter in the Hall

*(**TELEMACHUS** [**M3**] enters with Odysseus' bow. Suitors follow.)*

M3-TELEMACHUS. Okay, whose first?

SUITORS. ME! I'll go! Then me!

(He hands the bow to the suitors who struggle greatly and never come close to stringing it. **TELEMACHUS** *goes aside to* **ODYSSEUS**.*)*

M2-ODYSSEUS. Have you hidden all the weapons?

M3-TELEMACHUS. Yes. And the loyal swineherd is prepared to lock the doors from the outside. The loyal maid is taking all the women to a safe room. Mother is in her room, safe as well.

M2-ODYSSEUS. Then now is the time. I shall try to string the bow.

SUITORS. *(laughing)* By all means. Go right ahead.

(They hand him the bow. He strings it easily, mimes pulling an arrow and shoots it straight through the throat of a suitor. He has the arrow through the head around his throat. There is a gasp from the group as the suitor falls and the actor jumps away staring at the "body.")

M2-ODYSSEUS. *(removing disguise)* I am Odysseus!

(Another collective gasp. He then begins shooting arrows and all the other actors as suitors die by using blood stick props, then running to a new spot. Odysseus can even shoot a few of the people in the front row. There is much screaming as appropriate until finally Odysseus is done. Left alone on stage with bodies strewn about. **SUITOR** *[***M3***] turns into* **TELEMACHUS** *as appropriate.)*

M2-ODYSSEUS. I am victorious! Telemachus, my son, you fought bravely today.

M3-TELEMACHUS. Thank you father. I killed 3 or 4 of the 108 suitors.

M2-ODYSSEUS. *(patronizingly)* Very good. Clean this mess up. I'm going to see your mother.

*(***M1, M3*** and* **F2** *all sit onstage watching the final exchange.)*

The Great Bed

M2-ODYSSEUS. Penelope. It is I, Odysseus.

F1-PENELOPE. How can I be sure? You look exactly the same as when you left. Even better in fact, but that was 20 years ago.

M2-ODYSSEUS. And you look even better than when I left. More beautiful and charming and radiant. Surely the Goddess Athena has made us appear to each other as we dreamt for our reunion.

F1-PENELOPE. I'm still not sure.

M2-ODYSSEUS. What do I have to do to convince you it is me?

F1-PENELOPE. There are several tests I have to prove you are the true Odysseus and not a Faux-dysseus. Blood Sample, DNA, urine and stool…

(The other cast clear their throats and gesture to the clock!!!)

F1-PENELOPE. I shall have my bed *moved* to a room for you, while I think.

M2-ODYSSEUS. You shall not! **I** made that bed with my bare hands, out of a living olive tree and I built our bed chamber *around* it. If you move any bed, it is not the bed I built.

F1-PENELOPE. Odysseus, it's you!!! I knew only the true Odysseus would know about our bed! I love you so!

M2-ODYSSEUS. And I love you! Home at last!

The Ending

F2. And that covers it all!

M3. The Iliad,

M1. The Odyssey,

ALL. And All of Greek Mythology! *(gestures to clock)* in 99 minutes or less.

(**M1** *stops the timer with seconds to spare. They all sigh.)*

Blackout / The End

COSTUME & PROPERTY PLOT

General Costumes
Cast all wear:

- matching 2-shoulder below the knee white togas each with a different colored sash
- brown leather sandals

Cast props
- timer onstage
- Greek Idol sign [set onstage for Act II]
- Dry Erase board w/marker and eraser on easel [Set onstage for Act II]
- Semele wig *(Audience volunteer)*
- Semele sash *(Audience volunteer)*
- Baby Dionysus w/grapes and toga *(Audience volunteer)*
- random props used by soldiers climbing out of Trojan Horse {cup, flashlight, helmet, rubber chicken, pots & pans, whoopee cushion, etc...}*(Greek soldiers)*
- 12+ Ken dolls dressed as Greek soldiers *(Odysseus and his men)*

M1 Props
- lightning bolt *(Zeus)* [1 backstage/1 preset onstage]
- golden sandals {retrieved for Hera} *(Zeus)*
- flashlight *(Zeus)* [preset onstage]
- trident *(Poseidon)*
- black tape for finger moustache disguise *(Poseidon)*
- microphone *(Tom)*
- clip-on tie *(Tom)*
- large instruction manual *(Epimetheus)*
- 1 male crown *(Menelaos)* [preset onstage]
- 1 cell phone *(Menelaos)* [preset onstage]
- gun *(Menelaos)*
- camp chair or short column *(Achilles)* [preset onstage/struck after Act I]
- small 1 or 2 lb. dumbbell *(Achilles)* [preset onstage]
- dress and possible wig {Achillita disguise} *(Achilles)*
- sword *(Achilles)*
- shield *(Achilles)*
- cane *(Nestor)*
- eagle w/snakes in its talons on a stick */***M1***/*
- lyre *(Orpheus)*

– chisel *(Pygmalion)*
– Trojan helmet *(Trojan officer)*
– monocle *(Trojan officer)*
– sword *(Trojan officer)*
– Cyclops swim mask *(Cyclops)*
– dog ears *(Old Dog)*
– blood stick {end of arrow with red ribbon} *(Suitor)*

M2 props
– visor & programs *[***M2***]*
– cow nose *(Hera)*
– peacock feather *(Hera)*
– script page {dialogue for audience member} *(Hera)*
– crown {bribe for Paris}*(Hera)*
– Helmet of Invisibility {Helmet on a stick} *(Hades)*
– trident *(Hades)*
– 2 black hobby horses *(Hades)*
– laurel wreath *(Apollo)*
– lyre w/electric amp jack *(Apollo)*
– Norse helmet *(Thor)*
– Thor's hammer *(Thor)*
– lighter *(Prometheus)*
– roll of blue painters tape {divide stage at Iliad}[preset onstage]
– eyeglasses {to look wise}*(Odysseus)*
– sword *(Odysseus)*
– 1 Ken doll dressed as Odysseus *(Odysseus)*
– leather wine flask *(Odysseus)*
– 1 suction cup arrow *(Odysseus' men for Cyclops mask)*
– sword *(Hector)*
– shield *(Hector)*
– Trojan helmet *(Trojan soldier)*
– beer can in cozy *(Ares)*
– flannel shirt/coat {or John Deere cap or other appropriate redneck attire} *(Ares)*
– microphone *(Narrator)*
– ball of twine *(Ariadne)*

M3 props
– amp and chord *(Roadie)*
– Vulcan ears *(Hephaestus)*
– horn-rimmed glasses *(Hephaestus)*
– sword for forging *(Hephaestus in Iliad)*
– winged helmet *(Hermes)*
– caduceus *(Hermes)*
– sword {gift to Perseus in Greek Idol} *(Hermes)*
– Athena's shield {gift for Perseus in Greek Idol} *(Hermes)*
– box {gift for Perseus in Greek Idol} *(Hermes)*
– flowers {for Odysseus before facing Circe} *(Hermes)*
– 1 newspaper *(Man)* [preset onstage]

- 1 golden apple *(Eris)* [preset onstage]
- 1 backpack w/stuffed sheep hanging out*(Paris)* [preset onstage]
- Trojan armor {breastplate/helmet/shield & sword all worn askew} *(Paris)*
- crown *(Agamemnon)*
- sword *(Agamemnon)*
- arrow through the head {for Land of the Dead} *(Agamemnon)*
- sword *(Diomedes)*
- armor {old football shoulder pads and string} *(Diomedes)*
- sword *(Trojan lackey)*
- Trojan helmet *(Trojan lackey)*
- Trojan helmet *(Trojan soldier/guard)*
- sword *(Trojan soldier/guard)*
- sword *(Greek soldier)*
- cups {handed to Achilles and Hector as they run a marathon around the city} */***M3***/*
- Golden Fleece *(Jason)*
- bull horns *(Minotaur)*
- black hobby horse *(chariot horse)*
- Styrofoam cup *(Hercules)*
- baseball cap *(Coach Oedipus)*
- bag o' wind *(Aeolus)*
- tin with beeswax *(Odysseus crewman)* [preset onstage]
- crown *(King)*
- Odysseus' unstrung bow *(Telemachus)*
- arrow through the head for neck *(Suitor)*
- blood stick {end of arrow w/red ribbon} *(Suitor)*

F1 props
- microphone *(Jane)*
- Athena's helmet *(Athena)*
- Athena's shield *(Athena)*
- graduation mortarboard {bribe for Paris} *(Athena)*
- bow and arrow {gift to Pandaros to restart war} *(Athena)*
- beggar shawl {gift to Odysseus} *(Athena)*
- tasty looking plate of sacrifice covered in satin *(Carol)*
- unappealing looking plate of sacrifice covered in burlap *(Carol)*
- Pandora's box *(Carol)*
- key on a string for Pandora's box *(Carol)*
- wreath of autumn *(Demeter)*
- fright wig {bald w/hair on sides) *(Oracle)*
- blueprints *(Antenor)*
- Greek helmet *(Patroklos)*
- sword *(Patroklos)*
- sword *(Trojan Commander)*
- giant hobby horse *(Noble Steed)*
- microphone *(Announcer)*
- machete *(Medea)*

– green-faced head w/snakes for hair *(Medusa)*
– black hobby horse *(chariot horse)*
– baseball cap *(Coach Tantalus)*
– Greek helmet *(Greek soldier left behind)*
– wand *(Circe)*
– dark sunglasses *(Tiresias)*
– attractive wig *(Penelope)*
– blood stick {end of arrow w/red ribbon} *(Suitor)*

F2 props
– golden egg w/ wings on a stick *[***F2***]*
– camouflage bandana *(Artemis)*
– bow *(Artemis)*
– dead bunny *(Artemis)*
– cardigan w/ Greek Letters Alpha Rho Delta *(Aphrodite)*
– scroll/centerfold of Helen of Troy {bribe for Paris} *(Aphrodite)*
– blanket {thick mist to guide Paris to safety} *(Aphrodite)*
– magic wand {for Pygmalion in Agape Connection} *(Aphrodite)*
– apron *(Hestia)*
– pearl necklace *(Hestia)*
– white gloves *(Hestia)*
– hair band *(Pandora)*
– wreath/lei of daisies *(Persephone)*
– 2 matching crowns *(Helen)* [preset onstage]
– fishnet *(Thetis)*
– crown *(King Priam)*
– cane *(King Priam)*
– Trojan helmet *(Pandaros)*
– book {The Iliad} *(Narrator)*
– Trojan helmet *(Glaukos)*
– shield *(Glaukos)*
– sword *(Glaukos)*
– FedEx baseball cap *(Iris)*
– scroll {message for Hera} *(Iris)*
– Trojan helmet *(Trojan soldier)*
– sword *(Trojan soldier)*
– Trojan helmet *(Agenor)*
– beanie cap *(Phaethon)*
– microphone *(Announcer)*
– shawl (Odysseus' mother)
– Rasta wig (Calypso)
– coconut bra (Calypso)
– crown (Queen)
– blood stick {End of arrow w/ red ribbon} (Suitor)

(Obviously swords, shields, Greek and Trojan helmets can be shared. Original production used 6 matching swords, 2 shields, 2 Greek helmets and 2 Trojan helmets)

Character Breakdowns (in order of appearance - some played multiple times)

M1	**M2**	**M3**	**F1**	**F2**
M1	M2	M3	F1	F2
Zeus	Hera	Roadie	Jane	Artemis
Poseidon	Hades	Hephaestus	Athena	Aphrodite
Tom	Apollo	Hermes	Carol	Hestia
Epimetheus	Thor	Man	Demeter	Pandora
Sky	Prometheus	Wind	Drunken Woman	Persephone
Greek Chorus	Drunken Man	Drunken Man	Greek Chorus	Drunken Woman
Student	Greek Chorus	Greek Chorus	Ms. Henderson	Greek Chorus
Menelaos	Student	Student	Oracle	Student
Achilles	Principal Thomas	Narrator	Narrator	Helen
Narrator	Odysseus	Eris	Andromache	Iphigenia
Nestor	Hector	Paris	Antenor	Thetis
Ajax	Trojan Soldier	Agamemnon	Sleeping Trojan	Greek Soldier
Sleeping Trojan	Ares	Father	Patroklos	King Priam
Orpheus	Narrator	Diomedes	Trojan Commander	Pandaros
Pygmalion	Pyramus	Trojan Lackey	Noble Steed	Narrator
Peleus	Ariadne	Trojan Soldier	River God	Glaukos
Perseus	Sisyphus	Greek Soldier	Eurydice	Iris
Announcer		Exploitatis	Galatea	Trojan Soldier
Locker Room Guy		Jason	Announcer	Agenor
Trojan Officer		Minotaur	Medea	Thisbe
Greek Soldier		Midas	Medusa	Aescilapius
Odysseus Crewman		Chariot Horse	Theseus	Phaethon
Cyclops		Hercules	Chariot Horse	Announcer
Old Dog		Oedipus	Coach Tantalus	Odysseus Crewman
Suitor		Trojan Guard	Greek Soldier	Odysseus' Mother
		Odysseus Crewman	Odysseus Crewman	Calypso
		Aeolus	Circe	Queen
		King	Tiresias	Suitor
		Telemachus	Penelope	
		Suitor	Suitor	

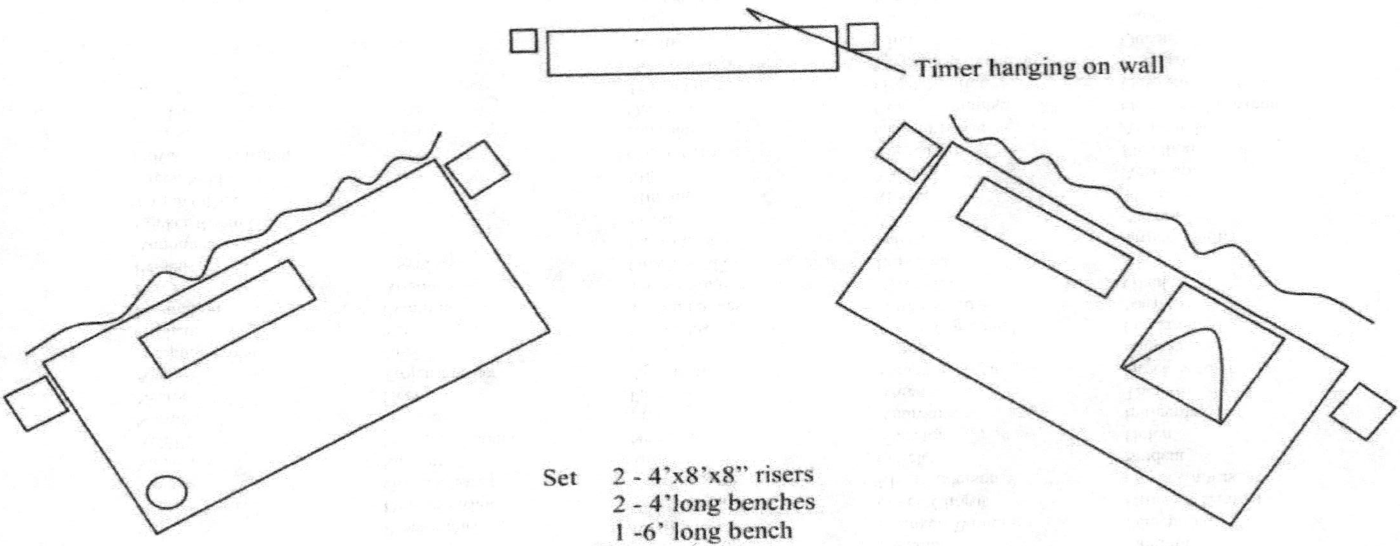

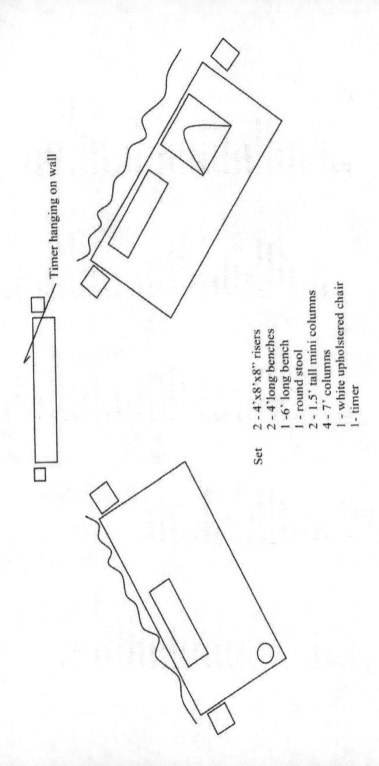

Set
2 - 4'x8'x8" risers
2 - 4'long benches
1 -6' long bench
1 - round stool
2 - 1.5' tall mini columns
4 - 7' columns
1 - white upholstered chair
1- timer

From the Reviews of

THE ILIAD, THE ODYSSEY & ALL OF GREEK MYTHOLOGY IN 99 MINUTES OR LESS ...

"...this riotous distillation of classic Greek mythology and Homer's epic poems takes boldface names from myth and literature and turns them into a thing that would make Cliffs-Notes and *Monty Python* proud....Hunter and Hopkins use pop culture to spoof some of the more overly dramatic Greek moments and do a wonderful job of picking up on all the things that never made sense in these traditional stories....

- Rebecca Swain, *Orlando Sentinel*